HTML

TOP 100

Simplified®

Tips & Tricks

by Paul Whitehead

From
maranGraphics®

&

Wiley Publishing, Inc.

192664

Visual

HTML: Top 100 Simplified® Tips & Tricks

Published by
Wiley Publishing, Inc.
111 River Street
Hoboken, NJ 07030
Published simultaneously in Canada

Copyright © 2003 by Wiley Publishing, Inc.,
Indianapolis, Indiana

Certain designs, text, and illustrations Copyright ©
1992-2003 maranGraphics, Inc., used with
maranGraphics permission.

maranGraphics, Inc.
5755 Coopers Avenue
Mississauga, Ontario, Canada
L4Z 1R9

Library of Congress Control Number:
ISBN: 0-7645-4211-7
Manufactured in the United States of America
10 9 8 7 6 5 4 3 2 1
1K/QV/QY/QT/IN

Trademark Acknowledgments

Important Numbers

For U.S. corporate orders, please call maranGraphics at
800-469-6616 or fax 905-890-9434.

For general information on our other products and
services or to obtain technical support please contact
our Customer Care Department within the U.S. at
800-762-2974, outside the U.S. at 317-572-3993 or
fax 317-572-4002.

Permissions

Wiley Publishing, Inc. is a trademark of Wiley Publishing, Inc.

U.S. Corporate Sales	U.S. Trade Sales
Contact maranGraphics at (800) 469-6616 or fax (905) 890-9434.	Contact Wiley at (800) 762-2974 or fax (317) 572-4002.

CREDITS

Project Editor:
Maureen Spears

Acquisitions Editor:
Jody Lefevere

Product Development Manager:
Lindsay Sandman

Copy Editor:
Marylouise Wiack

Technical Editor:
Kyle Bowen

Editorial Manager:
Rev Mengle

Permissions Editor:
Carmen Krikorian

Editorial Assistant:
Adrienne Porter

Manufacturing:
Allan Conley, Linda Cook,
Paul Gilchrist, Jennifer Guynn

Book Design:
maranGraphics, Inc.

Production Coordinator:
Mardiee Ennis

Layout:
LeAndra Hosier, Kristin McMullan,
Kathie S. Schnorr

Screen Artist:
Jill A. Proll

Proofreader:
Christine Pingleton

Quality Control:
Susan Moritz, Dwight Ramsey

Indexer:
Steve Rath

Vice President and Executive Group Publisher:
Richard Swadley

Vice President and Publisher:
Barry Pruett

Composition Director:
Debbie Stailey

ABOUT THE AUTHOR

Paul Whitehead is a computer consultant based in Toronto, Canada. He is the author of many books including Java and XML: Your Visual blueprint for creating Java-enhanced Web programs, available from Wiley Publishing and maranGraphics.

maranGraphics is a family-run business
located near Toronto, Canada.

At **maranGraphics**, we believe in producing great computer books—one book at a time.

Each maranGraphics book uses the award-winning communication process that we have been developing over the last 28 years. Using this process, we organize screen shots and text in a way that makes it easy for you to learn new concepts and tasks.

We spend hours deciding the best way to perform each task, so you don't have to! Our clear, easy-to-follow screen shots and instructions walk you through each task from beginning to end.

We want to thank you for purchasing what we feel are the best computer books money can buy. We hope you enjoy using this book as much as we enjoyed creating it!

Sincerely,

The Maran Family

Please visit us on the Web at:
www.maran.com

HOW TO USE THIS BOOK

HTML: Top 100 Simplified® Tips & Tricks includes the 100 most interesting and useful tasks you can perform using HTML. This book reveals cool secrets and timesaving tricks guaranteed to make you more productive.

Who is this book for?

Are you a visual learner who already knows the basics of HTML, but wants to take your HTML experience to the next level? Then this is the book for you.

Conventions In This Book

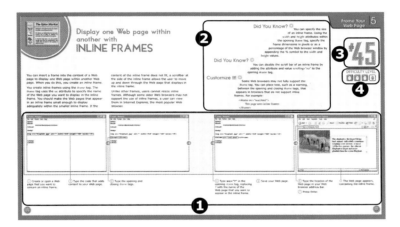

❶ Steps

This book walks you through each task using a step-by-step approach. Lines and "lassos" connect the screen sbots to the step-by-step instructions to show you exactly how to perform each task.

❷ Tips

Fun and practical tips answer questions you have always wondered about. Plus, learn to do things in <Topic> that you never through were possible!

❸ Task Numbers

The task numbers, ranging from 1 to 100, indicate which self-contained lesson you are currently working on.

❹ Difficulty Levels

For quick reference, symbols mark the difficulty level of each task.

Demonstrates a new spin on a common task

Introduces a new skill or a new task

Combines multiple skills requiring in-depth knowledge

Requires extensive skill and may involve other technologies

TABLE OF CONTENTS

1 Get Your Message Across with Text

2 Maximize the Impact of Your Web Page

3 Increase the Effectiveness of Your Links

4 Jazz Up Your Site with Multimedia

5 Frame Your Web Page

TABLE OF **CONTENTS**

⑥ Get Interactive with Forms

⑦ Better Organize Your Data with Lists

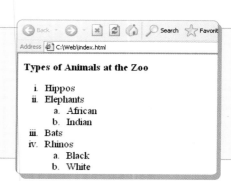

⑧ Arrange Your Objects Using Tables

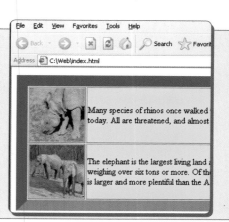

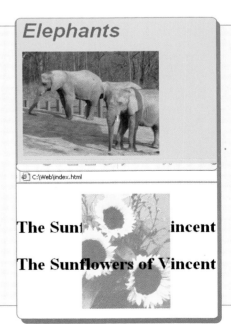

CHAPTER 1

Get Your Message Across with Text

Text is the foundation of almost every Web page on the World Wide Web. While images and animation are easier to manipulate and change, you can also manipulate plain text to improve its appearance, to draw attention to important areas of your Web pages, or to simply provide the user with more information about your Web pages.

You can identify a paragraph of text by enclosing it in the HTML paragraph tag p. You can change the text characteristics, such as alignment, by changing the attributes of the p tag.

The font tag is the most commonly used tag for changing the appearance and size of text on a Web page. The font tag allows you to easily alter the size, color, and type of font on a Web page.

While standard HTML tags allow you to change the appearance of individual sections of text on a Web page, you can create consistent, global text effects by using style sheets or JavaScript code in conjunction with HTML code.

You can apply style sheet information to complete paragraphs of text by changing the properties of the paragraph tag p using a style attribute. For smaller sections of text, you can apply styles using the div tag to identify the text.

You can use JavaScript code to generate text items, such as information about a Web page, and insert the text into the HTML code that the Web browser uses to create the Web page.

TOP 100

```
<td>
<tbody> <thead> <tr>
   <table>
```

You can add shadows to text on your Web page to make important information, such as headings or titles, stand out from the other information on your Web page.

The paragraph tag p denotes a section of text in a Web page. You can add a style attribute to the p tag to manipulate the text appearance within the starting and ending p tags.

The style attribute consists of three parts; the height value indicates the height of the text effect, while the font-size value specifies the exact size of the font

to which you are applying the shadow. The height value does not increase the size of the text, but sets aside a specific area of the Web page into which the Web browser places the text effect. If the height is greater than the font size, a gap appears between the text effect and any objects underneath the text effect.

You must make the filter value shadow with one parameter, the color of the text shadow. You can make the shadow color any valid HTML color.

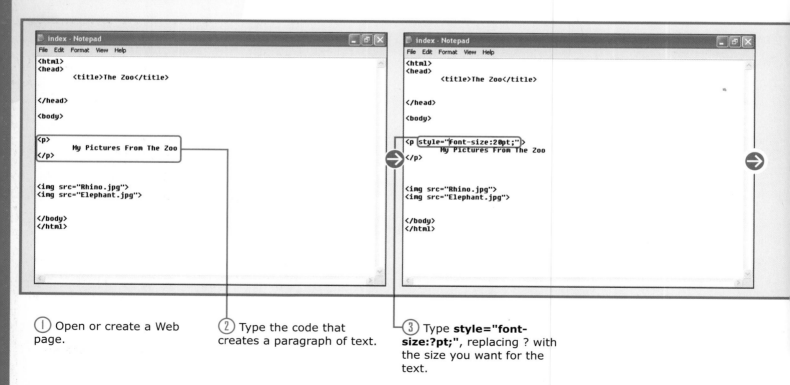

① Open or create a Web page.

② Type the code that creates a paragraph of text.

③ Type **style="font-size:?pt;"**, replacing ? with the size you want for the text.

Caution!

Many modern Web browsers, including Internet Explorer, support style sheets for effects such as the shadow filter. However, some browsers, particularly older ones, do not.

DIFFICULTY LEVEL

Apply It!

You can use any valid HTML color for the text shadow, but to be truly effective, you should make the color contrast with the Web page background. Valid colors include red, yellow, green, cyan, blue, magenta, black, and white. You can also specify HTML color codes, such as #FF0000 for red and #00FFFF for aqua.

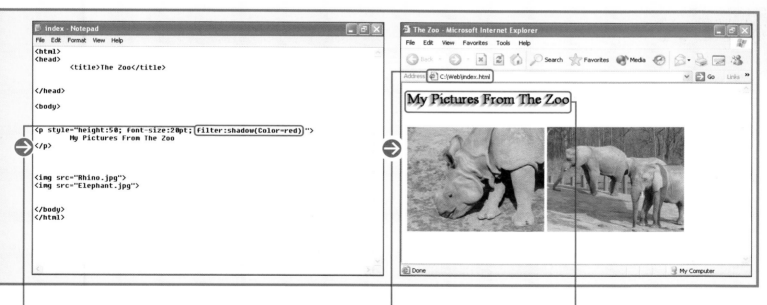

④ Type **filter:shadow(Color=?)**, replacing ? with the name or code of the color you want for the shadow.

⑤ Save your Web page.

⑥ Type the location of the Web page in your Web browser address bar.

⑦ Press Enter.

○ The shadow text appears.

SCROLLING TEXT EFFECTS

You can create a text effect that draws attention to an important part of your Web page and makes your Web page appear more dynamic.

The HTML tag marquee adds a moving text effect to your Web page. For example, you can use this effect to create a message that moves from one side of the Web page to another, similar to a ticker-tape display.

To create a scrolling text effect, the behavior attribute of the marquee tag must have a value of scroll. The direction attribute specifies the side of the

Web browser window towards which the text moves.

You can add a background color to the text effect to make the text stand out on the Web page. The bgcolor attribute indicates the background color, which should contrast with the text color for better readability.

You can specify the number of times the text displays using the loop attribute. By default, the text keeps looping indefinitely.

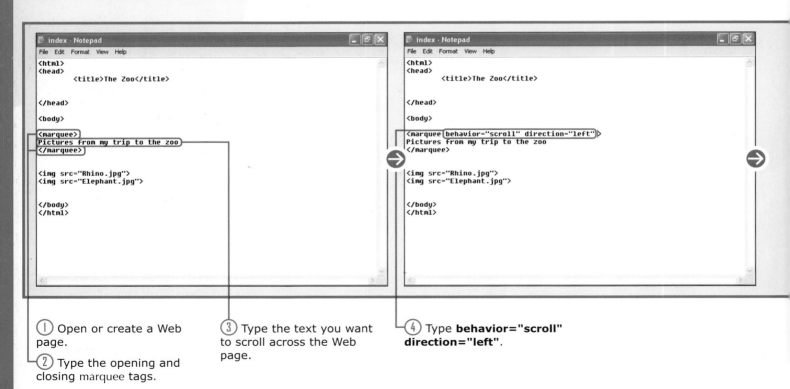

① Open or create a Web page.

② Type the opening and closing marquee tags.

③ Type the text you want to scroll across the Web page.

④ Type **behavior="scroll" direction="left"**.

Caution! ※

You should only use the marquee tag when you know that the people who are viewing your Web page have the Internet Explorer Web browser. This is because most other Web browsers do not support the marquee tag.

DIFFICULTY LEVEL

Apply It! ※

As well as side-to-side, you can also make your text move up or down. However, to be effective, scrolling text up or down may require a lot of area on your Web page. To move text from the top to the bottom of your Web browser window, specify up as the value for the direction attribute. For example:

<marquee behavior="scroll" direction="up">

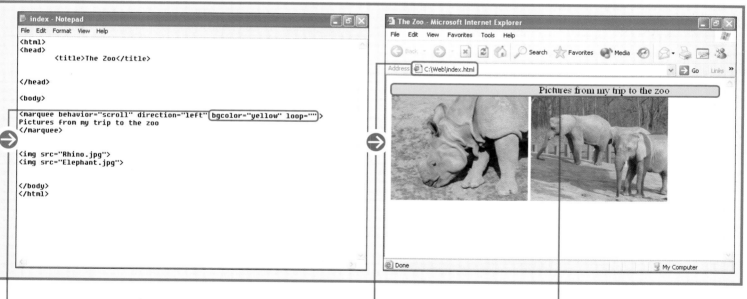

⑤ Type **bgcolor="?"**
loop="", replacing ? with the background color you want for the scrolling text.

⑥ Save your Web page.

⑦ Type the location of the Web page in your Web browser address bar.

⑧ Press Enter.

○ The text scrolls across the Web page.

You can display your Web page title as text in your Web page without having to retype it. This makes it easier to update your Web page, particularly if you use the title repeatedly in your Web page.

JavaScript allows you to access properties of the Web page, such as the title of the Web page. You can use a line of JavaScript code, enclosed within a pair of script tags, to access and generate the title of the document. The script tags tell the Web browser displaying the Web page that the enclosed code is JavaScript code and not standard HTML code.

JavaScript generates text using the document.write statement, followed by a set of parentheses. Whatever you place within the parentheses inserts into the HTML code when the Web page displays.

The JavaScript property that contains the title of the Web page is document.title. The Web browser displays the title using the document.write property to display the document.title property.

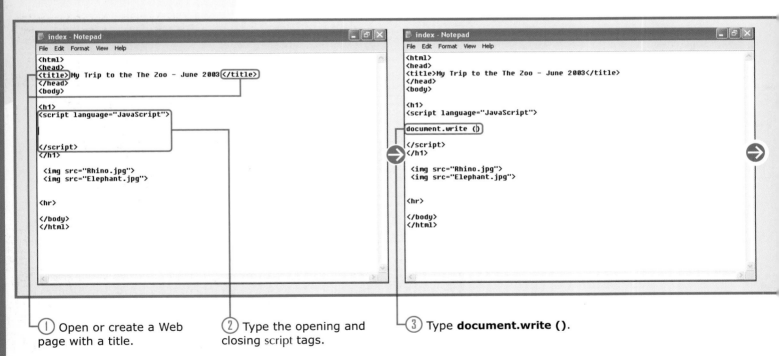

① Open or create a Web page with a title.

② Type the opening and closing script tags.

③ Type **document.write ()**.

Did You Know?

When you view a Web page, it may not be apparent whether the Web page contains all HTML code or some JavaScript code. To see if a Web page contains JavaScript code, you can view the source code of the Web page. All Web browsers allow a user to view the source code of a displayed Web page.

Apply It!

JavaScript uses the statement document.write to generate text. The document.write statement precedes a set of parentheses, (). A Web browser inserts any text in the parentheses into the HTML code of the Web page. You need to enclose text information in quotes. Numbers do not need quotes:

document.write("My Web Page")document.write(45)

DIFFICULTY LEVEL

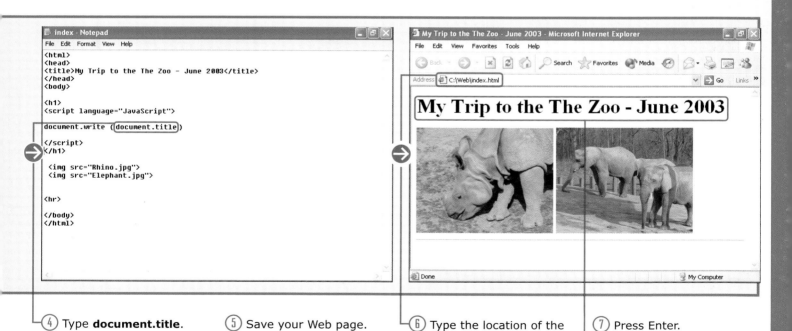

4) Type **document.title**.

5) Save your Web page.

6) Type the location of the Web page in your Web browser address bar.

7) Press Enter.

O The title of the Web page displays.

Display a
WEB PAGE FILENAME

You can insert the filename of a Web page into the text of the Web page. The filename of the Web page is the name with which you save the file, and not the title of the Web page.

Many Web pages display their filename at the bottom of the Web page along with other information, such as copyright and the last modification date. Having this information on your Web page makes it easier for users to identify it if they save or print it. It is especially beneficial to include this information on your Web page when it is dynamic or changes over time.

You can insert a small section of JavaScript code into the HTML code of your Web page to generate the filename of the Web page. The JavaScript property that stores the filename of the Web page is location.href. To display this information, you can use the document.write statement to insert the value of location.href into the HTML code.

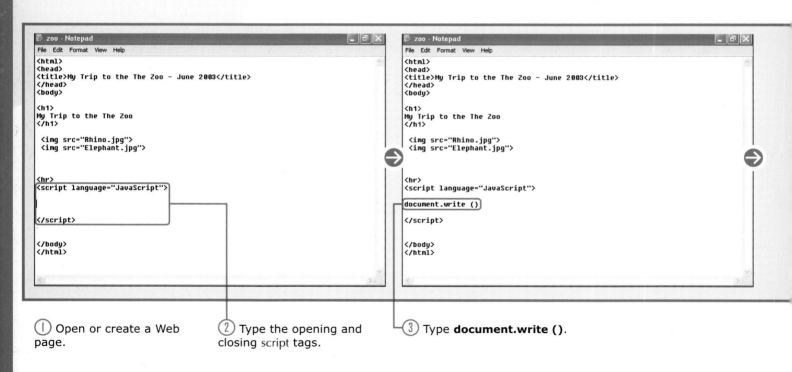

① Open or create a Web page.

② Type the opening and closing script tags.

③ Type **document.write ()**.

Apply It! ※

When displaying information on your Web page, you may want to include the name of the page that links to the current Web page. For example, if a user accesses your Web page with a search engine, you can display the name of the Web page for that search engine. A Web page that links to another Web page is called the *referrer*, and you can access the name of this page with the JavaScript property document.referrer:

```
<script language="JavaScript">
  document.write( document.referrer );
</script>
```

Did You Know? ※

If you want to apply formatting, such as text size or font color, to your Web page information, you can place the JavaScript script tags within the text formatting tags you want to use.

DIFFICULTY LEVEL

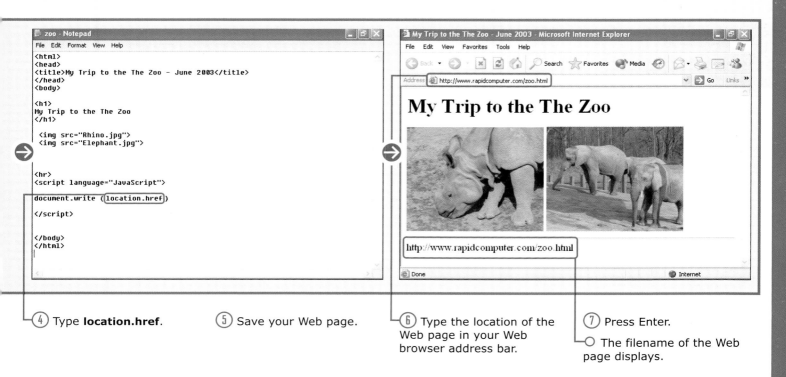

④ Type **location.href**.

⑤ Save your Web page.

⑥ Type the location of the Web page in your Web browser address bar.

⑦ Press Enter.

○ The filename of the Web page displays.

Add pizzazz by
MAKING TEXT GLOW

You can add a glowing effect to the text on your Web page. A glowing effect is a colored line that appears around the text's edges to make the text appear as if it were glowing. The colored line is not solid; it gradually fades out the farther it is from the center of the text. You can control the amount, or *intensity*, of fading effect to apply to the colored line.

You can use styles to create the glowing text effect. For example, if you apply the style attribute to a data cell in a table, the text effect applies to the text in the data cell.

The filter property lets you control different features of the glowing text. For example, you can select the color and relative strength of the glow. The higher the number that you specify for glow strength, the larger and more intense the glow effect is around the text.

The glowing text effect is most effective when you use a dark background on the Web page.

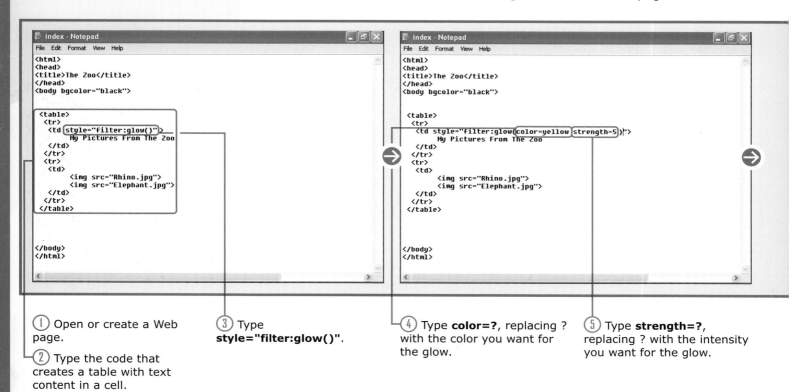

① Open or create a Web page.

② Type the code that creates a table with text content in a cell.

③ Type **style="filter:glow()"**.

④ Type **color=?**, replacing ? with the color you want for the glow.

⑤ Type **strength=?**, replacing ? with the intensity you want for the glow.

Did You Know? ※

The glowing text effect does not display in many older browsers. Fortunately, if a Web browser cannot display the text effect that you specify in the style attribute, the text still displays.

Apply It! ※

Adding a style to a data cell in a border also applies the style to the text in the cell. If the table has no border, the effect only applies to the text in the cell. You can create a border around the cell with the same text effect applied to the border by specifying a size for the border in the table tag using the border attribute:

```
<table border="0">
```

DIFFICULTY LEVEL

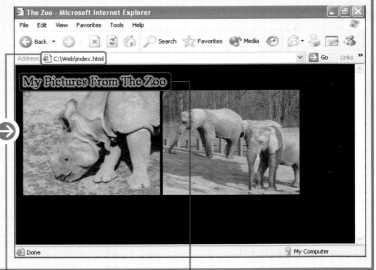

```
<html>
<head>
<title>The Zoo</title>
</head>
<body bgcolor="black">

<table>
<tr>
<td style="filter:glow( color=yellow strength=5);font-size:'18pt'">
   My Pictures From The Zoo
</td>
</tr>
<tr>
<td>
   <img src="Rhino.jpg">
   <img src="Elephant.jpg">
</td>
</tr>
</table>


</body>
</html>
```

⑥ Type **;font-size:'?'**, replacing ? with the size you want for the font.

⑦ Save your Web page.

⑧ Type the location of the Web page in your Web browser address bar.

⑨ Press Enter.

○ The text appears with a glowing effect.

13

Maximize the Impact of Your Web Page

Displaying Web pages is the primary purpose of a Web browser. The information about a Web page is stored in a text file comprised of *Hyper Text Markup Language*, simply referred to as HTML. The Web browser reads the HTML code from the text file and then the Web browser generates the components of the Web page in the Web browser window. The HTML file itself does not instruct the Web browser how to actually create the Web page; the Web browser itself determines how items appear. For example, a Web browser decides which background color to use if you do not specify one in the HTML code. Different Web browsers have different ways of creating, or *rendering*, items on a Web page. For example, Web browsers may display text in different fonts and sizes, depending on the Web browser in use.

You specify the components of a Web page using tags, which are simply keywords enclosed in brackets. For example, when an Web browser reads the tag <p> in an HTML file, it knows to add a blank line to start a new paragraph. Tags usually have a start and an end tag, with the end tag prefixing a forward slash before the tag name as in </p>.

Although there is a standard set of tags that all Web browsers should understand, you may have tags that are only specific to a particular Web browser. If a Web browser does not recognize a tag, the Web browser ignores the tag.

You can sometimes control how a Web browser reacts to a specific Web page component from within the HTML code of the Web page. You can specify the characteristics of backgrounds, margins, and rules and even change the behavior of the Web browser. For example, you can make the Web browser display a different Web page automatically. Web pages can allow users to interact with the Web browser, making tasks such as printing and adding favorites much easier for the user.

TOP 100

Stop the background from
SCROLLING

You can prevent a background image from moving within the Web browser window when a user scrolls through your Web page. Moving items give the impression that the content of the Web page is floating above the background image. When you use a fixed image as the background for a Web page, you refer to it as a *watermark* image.

You can use the background attribute of the body tag to indicate the name of the image you want to use as the background image. Once you specify the background image, you use the bgproperties attribute

to specify the image as static. The bgproperties attribute takes only one value, fixed. To stop the background from moving when a user scrolls through your Web page, you can simply omit the bgproperties attribute from the body tag.

If an image is smaller than the size of the Web browser window, the image displays repeatedly, or *tiles*. You can use the bgproperties attribute with either Web page-sized images or smaller images that tile.

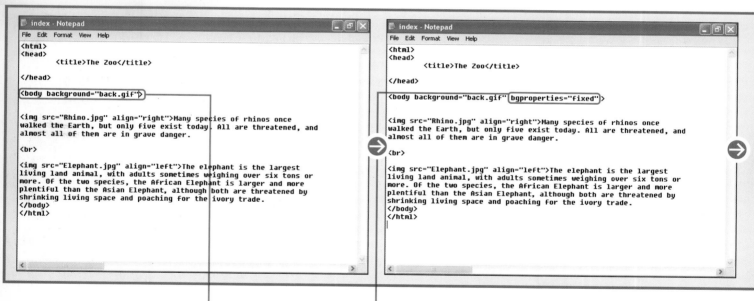

① Open or create a Web page in a text editor.

② Type the code that imports a background image for your Web page.

③ Type **bgproperties="fixed"**.

④ Save your Web page.

Did You Know? ※

You can use either .gif or .jpg images as your image background. Images in the .gif format are typically smaller and contain fewer colors than .jpg images, which are usually photographic images. When using a .jpg image, you should try to keep the image small. This prevents loading delays when the Web page displays.

Apply It! ※

As you create or acquire images to use as a Web page background, remember that you do not want the background images to obscure the content of the Web page. When you turn scrolling off, you cannot control the background area over which the page content appears. The best background images are small, dim, and in high contrast to the content of the Web page.

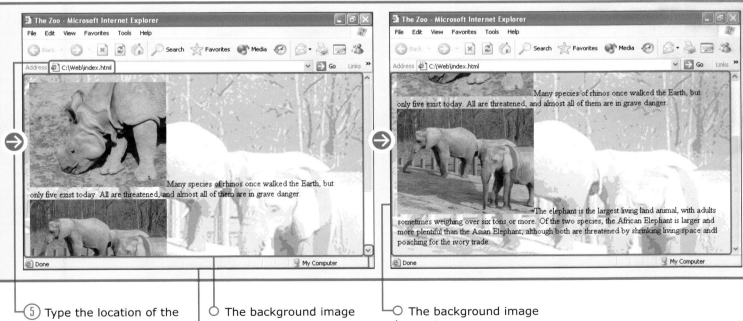

○ 5 Type the location of the Web page in your Web browser address bar.

○ 6 Press Enter.

○ The background image appears.

○ 7 Click the scroll bar down arrow to scroll down the Web page.

○ The background image does not move.

DESCRIBE WEB PAGES
to search engines

You can use HTML tags to describe your Web pages to search engines. Search engines automatically scan and search Web pages on the Web, cataloging and organizing them into easily searchable databases. Search engines use HTML meta tags to catalog your Web pages.

You insert meta tags into the head section of the Web page. Users viewing your Web page never see the information in the meta tags unless they view the source code of your Web page.

To create a meta tag, you can specify the type of meta tag you want as the value for the name attribute, and the information you want as the value for the content attribute.

You can use the description meta tag to describe your Web page to the search engine. You should make the description a short summary of the Web page, no longer than two sentences. The keyword meta tag allows you to specify individual words that pertain to your Web page. You should use only unique words within the keyword meta tag.

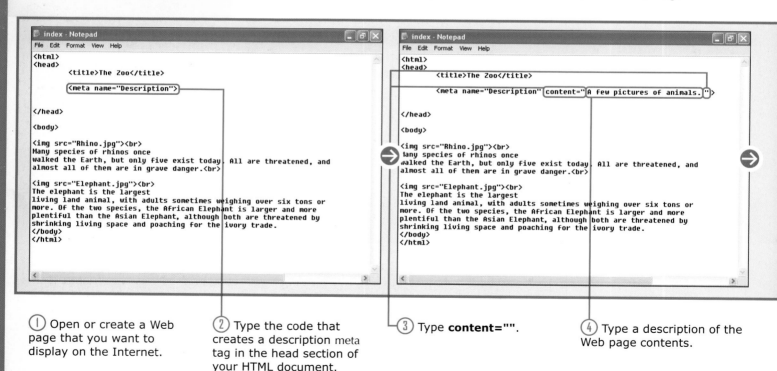

① Open or create a Web page that you want to display on the Internet.

② Type the code that creates a description meta tag in the head section of your HTML document.

③ Type **content=""**.

④ Type a description of the Web page contents.

Apply It! ※

Occasionally, you may not want
a search engine to scan and catalog
your Web page. You can use the robots
meta tag to tell a search engine not to
scan or follow any links on your Web page.
The meta tag to turn off search engine
cataloging is:

<meta name="robots" content="noindex,nofollow">

Search engines do not have to obey the robots meta
tag and may catalog your Web page, regardless of
your meta tag's instructions.

#7

DIFFICULTY LEVEL

Did You Know? ※

Regardless of the content of the meta tags in
your HTML code, search engines typically use
the titles and headings in your Web pages to
catalog them. Keep in mind that meta tags are
not a substitute for accurate and descriptive titles
and headings.

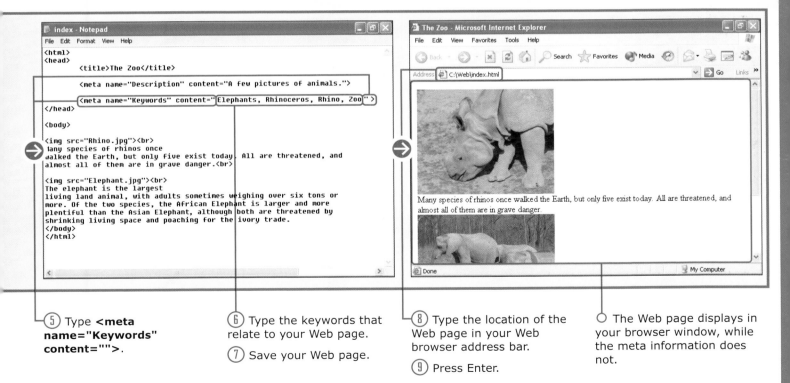

⑤ Type **<meta
name="Keywords"
content="">**.

⑥ Type the keywords that
relate to your Web page.

⑦ Save your Web page.

⑧ Type the location of the
Web page in your Web
browser address bar.

⑨ Press Enter.

○ The Web page displays in
your browser window, while
the meta information does
not.

Define the exact size of
MARGIN SPACING

You can specify the exact size of the margins that the Web browser places around the content of your Web pages.

A margin is the area of space between the side of the Web browser window and the items, such as images and text, which make up the content of your Web page. Larger margins can make the content of your Web page easier to read, and specifying margin width can help you control the layout of your Web page.

You can apply a style to the body tag of the Web page using the style attribute. You can then set values for the style attribute that specify margin widths around your Web page. You use the margin-left and margin-right properties to set the margins on the sides of the browser window, and the margin-top property to set the margin at the top of the window.

You can specify the margin width in pixels or as a percentage of the Web browser window.

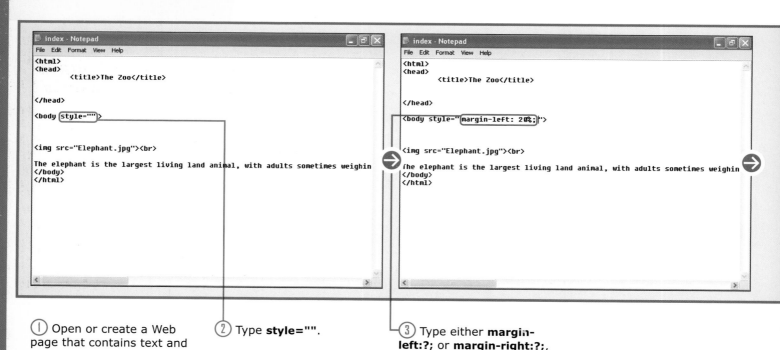

① Open or create a Web page that contains text and images.

② Type **style=""**.

③ Type either **margin-left:?;** or **margin-right:?;**, replacing ? with a width for the left or right margin.

#8

DIFFICULTY LEVEL

Apply It!

By using the attributes leftmargin and topmargin, you can use the body tag itself to specify the left and top margins.

`<body leftmargin="1" topmargin="2"`

Did You Know?

Margin width only applies to the content of a Web page, not the background. If you need to display information, such as a logo, in a margin, you can create a background image and place it behind the Web page content, where it extends into the space reserved for the margins.

Apply It!

You can easily specify one width for all margins on a Web page using the margin: value for the style attribute:

`style="margin: 100;"`

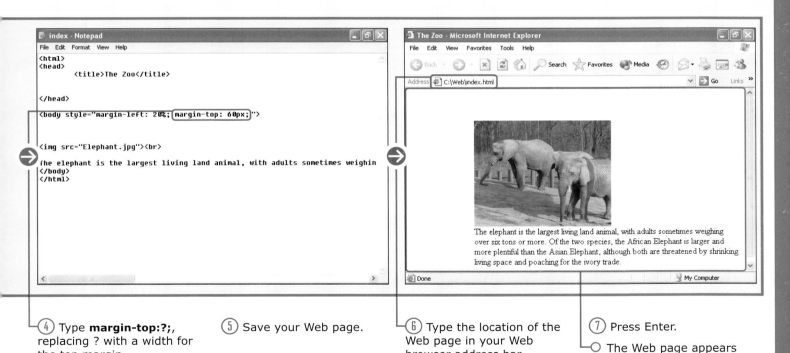

④ Type **margin-top:?;**, replacing ? with a width for the top margin.

⑤ Save your Web page.

⑥ Type the location of the Web page in your Web browser address bar.

⑦ Press Enter.

○ The Web page appears with the margins you specify.

DISPLAY A RULE
without a shade

A horizontal rule appears as a line across a Web page. You can use it to divide a Web page into sections or for purely aesthetic value.

Web browsers draw a horizontal rule using a three-dimensional effect that gives the appearance of the horizontal rule with a shadow. The actual appearance of the shadow may differ depending on the type of Web browser used to view the Web page. You can make a horizontal rule appear more like a standard line by removing the shadow effect of the horizontal rule.

To disable the three-dimensional effect of the horizontal rule, you can insert the noshade attribute into the hr tag. The noshade attribute does not have a value, so if you want to turn the shading effect back on, you must remove the noshade attribute from the hr tag.

You can specify the width of a horizontal rule as either a percentage of the width of the Web browser window, or more precisely using pixels.

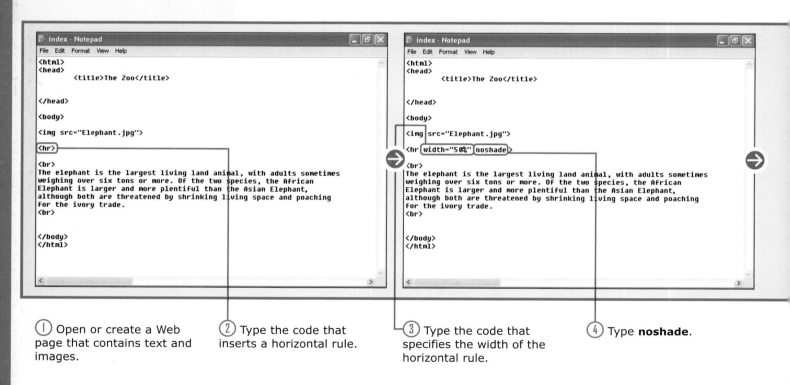

① Open or create a Web page that contains text and images.

② Type the code that inserts a horizontal rule.

③ Type the code that specifies the width of the horizontal rule.

④ Type **noshade**.

Apply It! ☀

You can use the align attribute to place a horizontal rule on either side of your Web page. By default, a horizontal rule appears on the left side of a Web page. To move it to the other side of your Web page, use the right value of the align attribute:

<hr align="right">

Apply It! ☀

The Internet Explorer Web browser also supports the color attribute of the hr tag. Not only does the color attribute change the color of the horizontal rule, it also turns off the shadow effect, making it unnecessary to use the noshade attribute.

⑤ Repeat steps **2** to **4** for each rule you want to add to your Web page.

⑥ Save your Web page.

⑦ Type the location of the Web page in your Web browser address bar.

⑧ Press Enter.

○ The horizontal rules appear without shadows.

RELOAD A WEB PAGE

You can force a Web page to reload after a specific period of time so that a Web page containing dynamic content can change periodically. Refreshing ensures that a user sees the most recent—not older, possibly outdated—information. For example, dynamic Web pages often contain weather or news information.

You can place a meta tag within the head section of a Web page to reload the Web page. You then set the http-equiv attribute to a value of refresh. Finally, you

can set the content attribute of the meta tag with the number of seconds that you want the Web page to appear before it reloads.

When specifying the number of seconds between reloading a Web page, you should give enough time for a user to read all the contents of the Web page. If the Web page is quite long, you should consider splitting the content among multiple Web pages.

Although you can use the meta tag to reload, you more commonly use it to redirect a user to a different page. For more on redirecting users, see task #12.

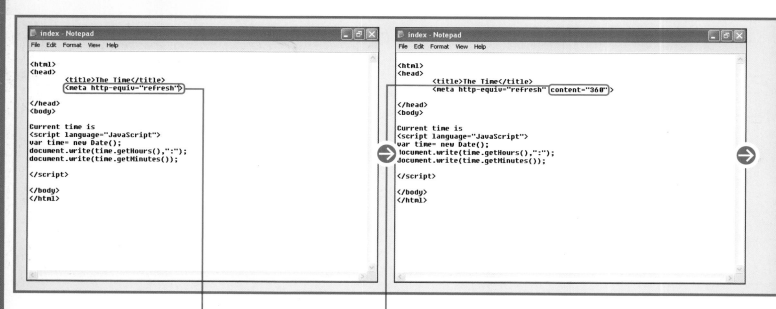

① Open or create a Web page.

○ This example uses a Web page that displays the current time.

② Type **<meta http-equiv="refresh">**.

③ Type **content="?"**, replacing ? with the number of seconds before your Web page refreshes.

④ Save your Web page.

24

DIFFICULTY LEVEL

Did You Know?

Even if you use a meta tag in your Web page to automatically reload it, users can still reload at any time by clicking their Web browser's reload feature.

Apply It!

When you set a Web page to automatically reload, consider including a warning on the page to notify the user about this setting. The Web page may go blank prior to reloading, and users may think they have a Web browser problem.

Apply It!

When the meta tag has the content attribute set to a value of 0, the Web page continuously reloads. While this ensures that the latest version of the Web page always displays, it is not a practical way of providing up-to-date information on a Web Page.

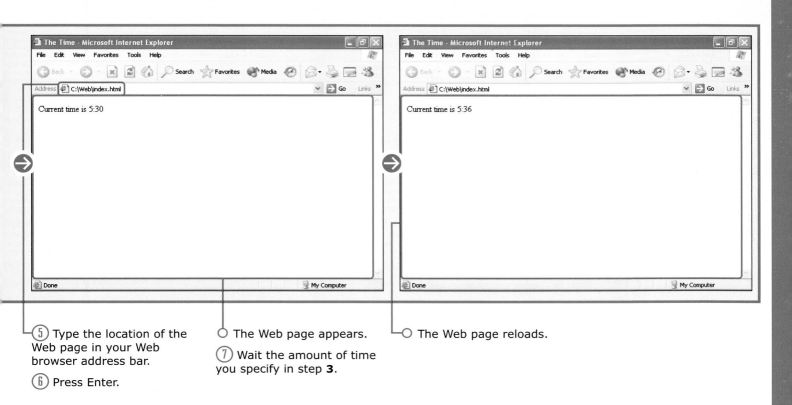

⑤ Type the location of the Web page in your Web browser address bar.

⑥ Press Enter.

○ The Web page appears.

⑦ Wait the amount of time you specify in step **3**.

○ The Web page reloads.

Using style blocks to
ALIGN PAGE ELEMENTS

One of the most difficult aspects of creating a Web page is ensuring that the alignment of items remains consistent when you view the page on different Web browsers or at different resolutions. You can use a *style block* to control the alignment of items on a Web page.

A style block is a section of code that contains alignment instructions. You can place it in the head section of your HTML code and then apply the alignment instruction to different items in the Web page.

A style block consists of a period, followed by the name of a style you create, and then the properties of that style. For alignment purposes, you can use the left property to specify how far to move items over from the left, and the position property with a relative value to move an item relative to the original position of the item on the Web page.

To assign a style that you create, you simply place a class attribute in the HTML tag and assign the name of your style as the value.

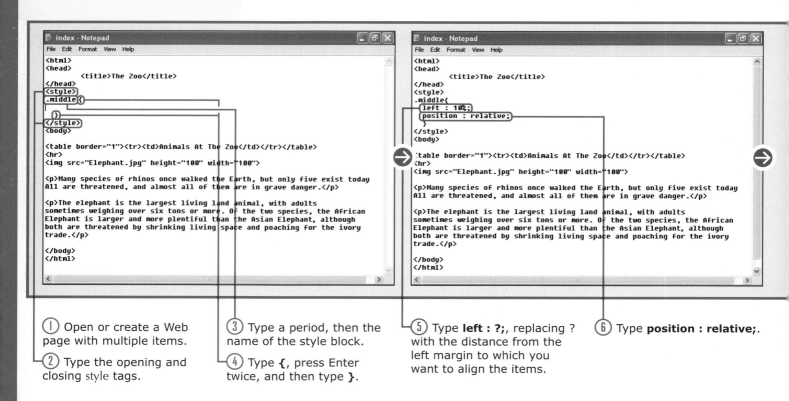

① Open or create a Web page with multiple items.

② Type the opening and closing style tags.

③ Type a period, then the name of the style block.

④ Type **{**, press Enter twice, and then type **}**.

⑤ Type **left : ?;**, replacing ? with the distance from the left margin to which you want to align the items.

⑥ Type **position : relative;**.

Apply It!

You can use the left property in a style block to align items on their left side, the most common type of alignment. You can also align items along their other sides:

Style Properties	
Property	*Alignment*
right	Align items from the right.
bottom	Align items from the bottom.
top	Align items at the top.

Apply It!

By default, the distance that you specify in the left property is in pixels. You can align items using a percentage by appending the percentage sign, %, to the value of the left property. The distance then becomes a percentage of the window width of the Web browser.

#11

DIFFICULTY LEVEL

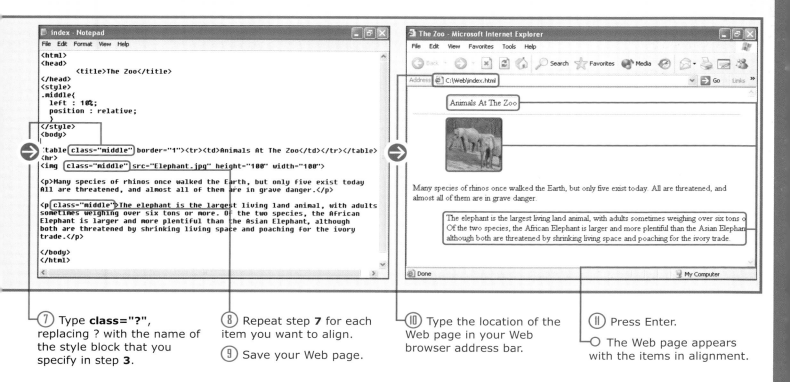

⑦ Type **class="?"**, replacing ? with the name of the style block that you specify in step **3**.

⑧ Repeat step **7** for each item you want to align.

⑨ Save your Web page.

⑩ Type the location of the Web page in your Web browser address bar.

⑪ Press Enter.

○ The Web page appears with the items in alignment.

REDIRECT USERS
to another Web page

When users load your Web page into their browser, you can automatically redirect them to another Web page.

For example, if you call the main page of your Web site company.html, you may want to create a Web page called index.html that automatically redirects users to the company.html Web page. Then, if users inadvertently try to load the file index.html, the most common name for Web pages on the Internet, instead of seeing a file-not-found error, they are redirected to the correct Web page on your site.

You can insert a single-line JavaScript script into the head section of the Web page that tells the Web browser to load another Web page. The JavaScript variable window.location stores the location of the current Web page that appears. By assigning a new value to this variable, which is the page to go to, you are instructing the Web browser to load that page.

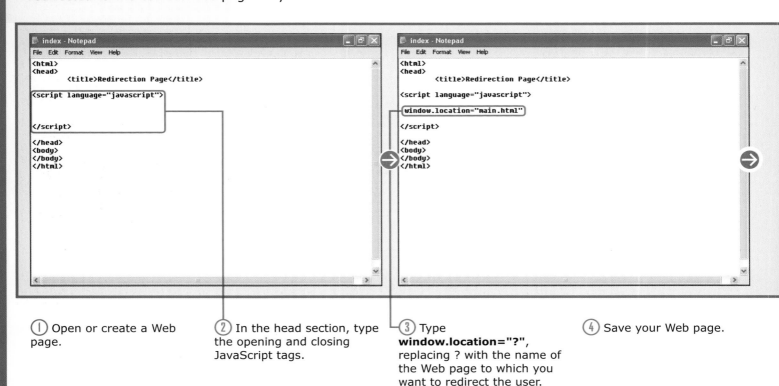

① Open or create a Web page.

② In the head section, type the opening and closing JavaScript tags.

③ Type **window.location="?"**, replacing ? with the name of the Web page to which you want to redirect the user.

④ Save your Web page.

#12

DIFFICULTY LEVEL

Did You Know?

You can redirect users to different Web pages when you change or rearrange content on your Web site. Instead of constantly informing users about where you have moved the content, you can automatically redirect the user to the content for which they are looking.

Apply It!

You can also redirect users to another Web page with the http-equiv meta tag, by setting the attribute url to the value of the new page. When you use this tag in conjunction with the reload timeout, it displays a page long enough for a user to read a message, and then redirects the user to the new page automatically. For more information about reloading Web pages, see task #10.

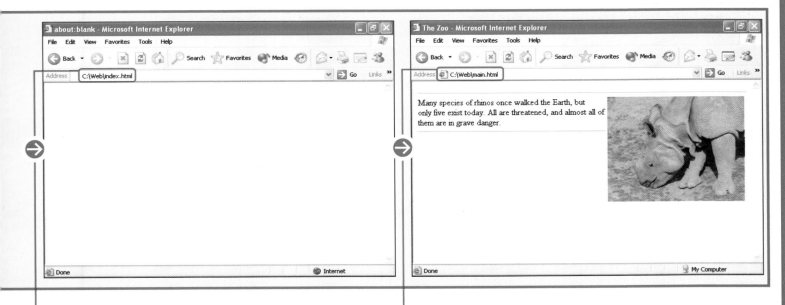

⑤ Type the location of the Web page in your Web browser address bar.

⑥ Press Enter.

○ The Web page appears, and the location changes.

Display a Web page's
LAST MODIFICATION DATE

You can display information about the last time you modified a Web page. Displaying this information helps users to determine how current the information on the Web page is. Displaying the last modified date and time of a Web page is more important for a Web page with changing content, such as a news page.

You can use a small line of JavaScript code to generate the date and time that you last saved the Web page. This date and time usually appears at the

bottom of the Web page. JavaScript uses the document.write() method to generate text, and the document.lastModified property to store the date and time when you last saved the Web page. You must enclose the JavaScript code within a starting and ending script tag.

The last modified date and time information actually indicates when you last saved the Web page to the Web server. The date and time information that appears is based on Greenwich Mean Time, GMT.

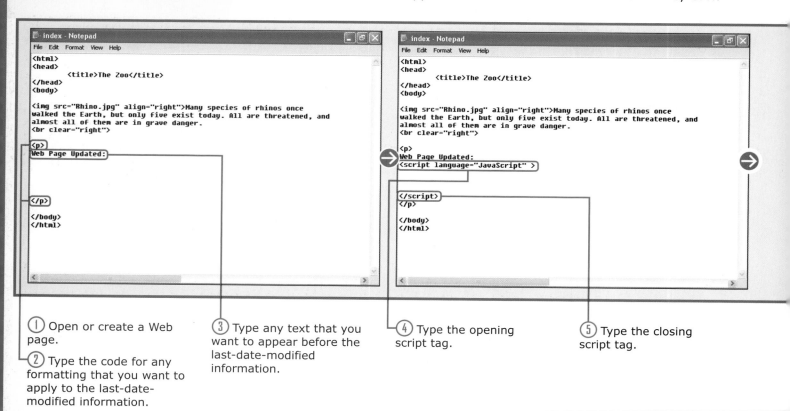

```
index - Notepad
File Edit Format View Help
<html>
<head>
        <title>The Zoo</title>
</head>
<body>

<img src="Rhino.jpg" align="right">Many species of rhinos once
walked the Earth, but only five exist today. All are threatened, and
almost all of them are in grave danger.
<br clear="right">

<p>
Web Page Updated:


</p>

</body>
</html>
```

```
index - Notepad
File Edit Format View Help
<html>
<head>
        <title>The Zoo</title>
</head>
<body>

<img src="Rhino.jpg" align="right">Many species of rhinos once
walked the Earth, but only five exist today. All are threatened, and
almost all of them are in grave danger.
<br clear="right">

<p>
Web Page Updated:
<script language="JavaScript" >

</script>
</p>

</body>
</html>
```

① Open or create a Web page.

② Type the code for any formatting that you want to apply to the last-date-modified information.

③ Type any text that you want to appear before the last-date-modified information.

④ Type the opening script tag.

⑤ Type the closing script tag.

Apply It! ☀

You do not have to make any
changes to a Web page to update
the last modified date and time
information. If you simply open the Web
page in a text editor and resave the Web
page without actually modifying it, the last
modified information still updates to reflect the
date and time you save the Web page.
Make sure that your Web server time is
correctly set before saving your Web
pages; otherwise, the last modified
information will be incorrect.

Customize It! ☀

You can encapsulate the JavaScript code that
generates the date and time information in any
standard HTML code. This means that you can apply
font formatting, change the text color, or even place
the date and time information in a table.

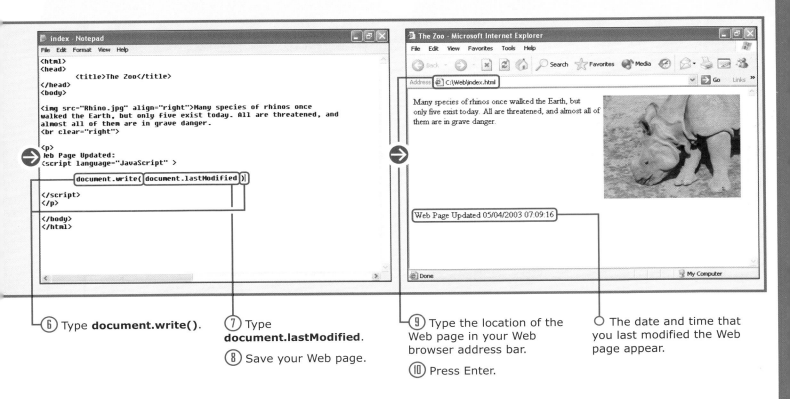

⑥ Type **document.write()**.

⑦ Type
document.lastModified.

⑧ Save your Web page.

⑨ Type the location of the
Web page in your Web
browser address bar.

⑩ Press Enter.

○ The date and time that
you last modified the Web
page appear.

Organize content with
VERTICAL LINES

You can create vertical lines in your Web page to organize content or to simply improve the Web page's appearance. You can use the hr tag to easily draw a horizontal line on a Web page. Although there is no HTML tag to draw a vertical line, you can use tables to insert vertical lines into your Web page.

To divide two pieces of content with a vertical line, you place the content into separate cells of a table. You then add a vertical line to a table cell that divides the cells holding your content.

You use a spacer tag to insert blank space into a table cell. A spacer itself is transparent, but if the table cell has a background color, the spacer appears as a vertical line extending from the top to the bottom of the table. You can specify the thickness of a spacer, and thus the thickness of the vertical line that appears on your Web page.

Although the spacer tag is not a standard HTML tag, Internet Explorer, the most common Web browser currently in use, does support it.

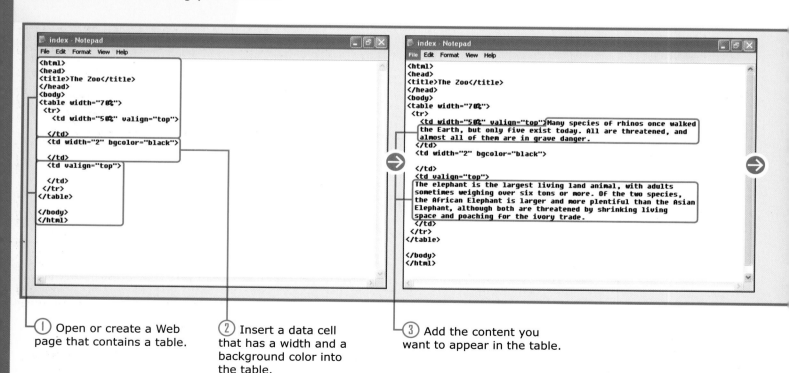

① Open or create a Web page that contains a table.

② Insert a data cell that has a width and a background color into the table.

③ Add the content you want to appear in the table.

 # 14

DIFFICULTY LEVEL

Customize It! ☀

You can alter the color of a vertical line by changing the background color of the table cell to which the spacer tag belongs.

Apply It! ☀

You can also use a graphic image as a vertical line. If the image is a solid color, you can adjust the size of the vertical line by specifying new values for the width and height attributes on the img tag that displays the line.

Customize It! ☀

You can use the size attribute of the spacer tag to adjust the size of the line. You can make the width of a line as small as one pixel, for a very thin line, or as wide as the Web page. For most scenarios, a width of a few pixels should suffice.

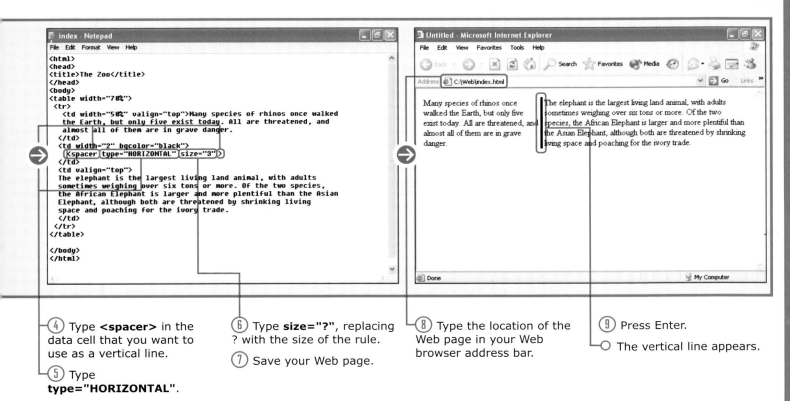

④ Type **<spacer>** in the data cell that you want to use as a vertical line.

⑤ Type **type="HORIZONTAL"**.

⑥ Type **size="?"**, replacing ? with the size of the rule.

⑦ Save your Web page.

⑧ Type the location of the Web page in your Web browser address bar.

⑨ Press Enter.

○ The vertical line appears.

Using a print button to
PRINT A WEB PAGE

You can place a print button on your Web page to allow users to quickly print your Web page. A print button is a very useful feature for Web pages that typically require printing, such as Web pages containing contracts, meeting agendas, or schedules.

To create a button, you use the input tag with an attribute set to a value of button. You can specify the text that you want to appear on the print button. The size of the button adjusts to fit the text you specify. Print buttons typically appear at the top or the bottom of your Web page.

Once you create the button, you can assign JavaScript code to it. The browser processes this code whenever a user clicks the button. The JavaScript code that displays a printer dialog box is window.print().

The printer dialog box does not actually print the Web page, but it does allow the user to select printing preferences, such as type of printer, and then to start printing.

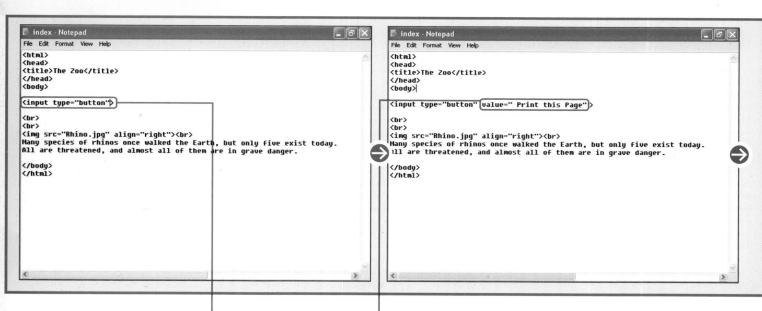

① Open or create a Web page that contains information you want to print.

② Type **<input type="button">**.

③ Type **value="?"**, replacing ? with the text that you want to appear on the button.

Did You Know? ☀

The text that appears on a
button should accurately reflect the
function of the button. Many users are
unfamiliar with print buttons on Web
pages and may confuse them with links or
form buttons. You should use very descriptive
text, such as "Printer Friendly Version" or
"Format Page for Printing," when creating the
text for the print button.

Customize It! ☀

You can use a text link as a print button
instead of an actual print button. For example,
you can use the onClick JavaScript property with
most HTML tags, including links. For example:

```
<a href="javascript:" onClick="window.print()">
        Print this Web Page
</a>
```

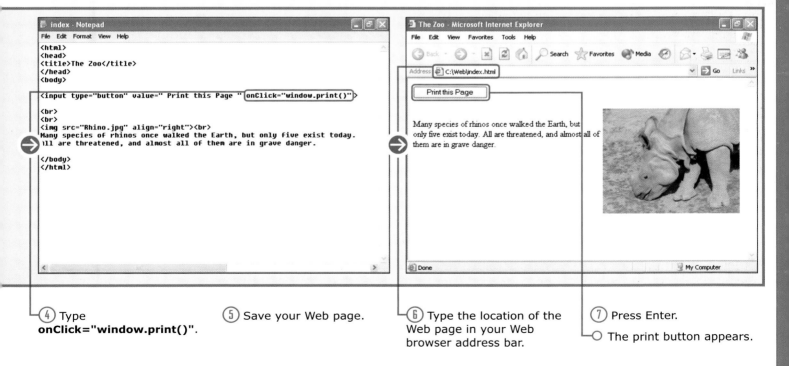

④ Type
onClick="window.print()".

⑤ Save your Web page.

⑥ Type the location of the
Web page in your Web
browser address bar.

⑦ Press Enter.

○ The print button appears.

Using styles to
PRINT SELECTED ITEMS

Web pages contain a wide range of content such as information, advertisements, and navigation buttons. When a user prints your Web page, you can specify which items in the Web page appear in the printout. For example, you may not want a user to print navigation buttons, as they are not necessary information in a printout.

You can use a style to determine what elements in a Web page appear when you view the Web page in different media. You can use the display property to

specify if an item to which you apply the style appears. To stop items from printing, the style simply notifies the browser that it should not print any element to which you apply the style.

You can use the @media type print in the style section to signify the media type to which you want to apply the style, in this case, print output. You can check the print preview of a Web page to see what items will print out.

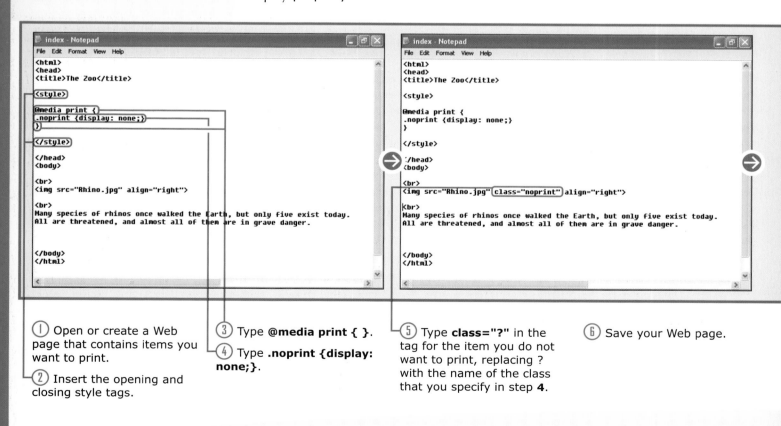

① Open or create a Web page that contains items you want to print.

② Insert the opening and closing style tags.

③ Type **@media print { }**.

④ Type **.noprint {display: none;}**.

⑤ Type **class="?"** in the tag for the item you do not want to print, replacing ? with the name of the class that you specify in step **4**.

⑥ Save your Web page.

Customize It! ※

You can also use the @media style block to select options that you want to apply to a Web page when you print it. For example, to increase the font size of text on a Web page to 14 pt, you use a style block with the font-size property of the body set to 14 pts:

```
@media print {
body {font-size: 14pt;}
    }
```

Apply It! ※

You can use different font characteristics for fonts that display on the screen versus those that you use for printing. For example, to use two different sized fonts, use:

```
@media print {
BODY { font-size: 10pt }
}
@media screen {
BODY { font-size: 16pt }
    }
```

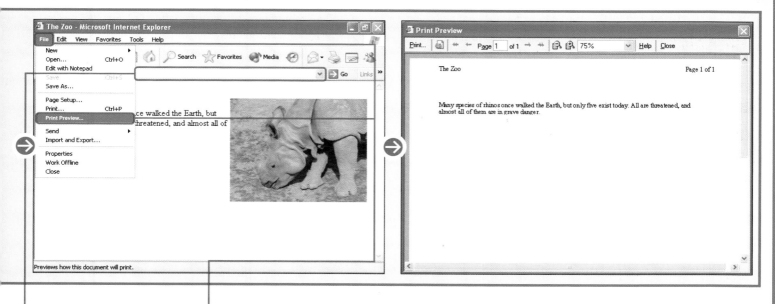

⑦ Type the location of the Web page in your Web browser address bar.

⑧ Press Enter.

⑨ Click File.

⑩ Click Print Preview.

○ A print preview of the Web page appears, showing only the items you select for printing.

ADD A PAGE TO FAVORITES

You can allow users to add your page to the list of favorites in their Web browser, making it easier for them to visit your Web page in the future. Users also refer to favorites as bookmarks.

You can use a line of JavaScript code to add the Web page to the list of favorites. Most Web browsers do not allow scripts running in a Web page to

automatically add themselves to the list of favorites. The Web browser should always ask the user to confirm the addition of new items to the favorites list.

You can use the input type to create a button that the user can click in order to add the Web page to the list of favorites. When you add this feature, you must specify the address of the Web page and the name to assign the Web page when it appears in the list of favorites.

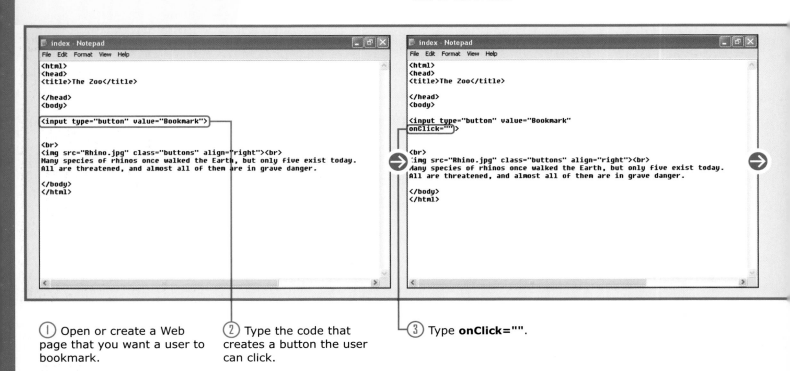

① Open or create a Web page that you want a user to bookmark.

② Type the code that creates a button the user can click.

③ Type **onClick=""**.

DIFFICULTY LEVEL

Apply It! ☀

For users to add your Web page to their bookmark list, you need to make the process easy. You also need to give them a good reason to add the page to their favorites by providing useful and constantly updated content on your Web page.

Customize It! ☀

You do not have to specify the name of the current Web page when adding a favorite. This is useful when you have a constantly changing Web site with a static main page. For example, on a Web site with news stories, you can place a link on each news article page. This allows the user to add the main news Web page, instead of the link to the article itself, to their favorites.

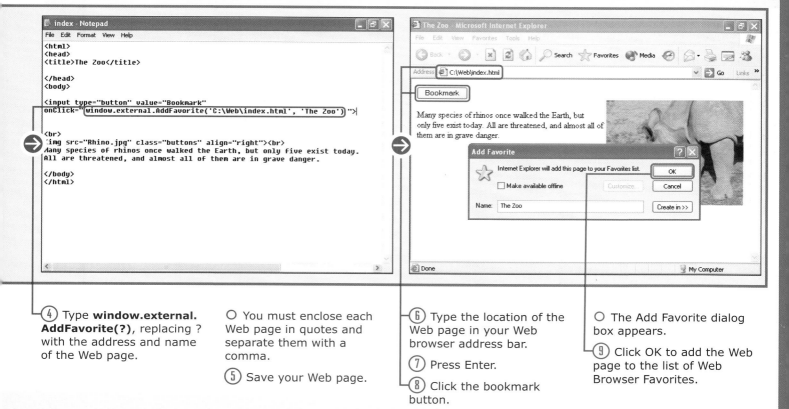

④ Type **window.external. AddFavorite(?)**, replacing ? with the address and name of the Web page.

○ You must enclose each Web page in quotes and separate them with a comma.

⑤ Save your Web page.

⑥ Type the location of the Web page in your Web browser address bar.

⑦ Press Enter.

⑧ Click the bookmark button.

○ The Add Favorite dialog box appears.

⑨ Click OK to add the Web page to the list of Web Browser Favorites.

Create
DYNAMIC BACKGROUND COLORS

You can let users change the background color of your Web page to a different color. Users can change the color to make the Web page easier to read on different displays, such as laptop screens, or they can change the color purely for aesthetic reasons. You must make background colors solid colors.

The simplest way to allow users to change the color of the background is to present them with an array of buttons, each button representing a different background color. You can create buttons using the input tag with the type attribute set to button. You

can assign the JavaScript code that changes the background color to the button. You store the color of the background in the JavaScript variable document.bgColor. Changing this variable changes the background color.

You should always specify a button that allows the user to change the background color back to the original color of the Web page. Alternatively, the user can reset the original background color by reloading the Web page in the Web browser.

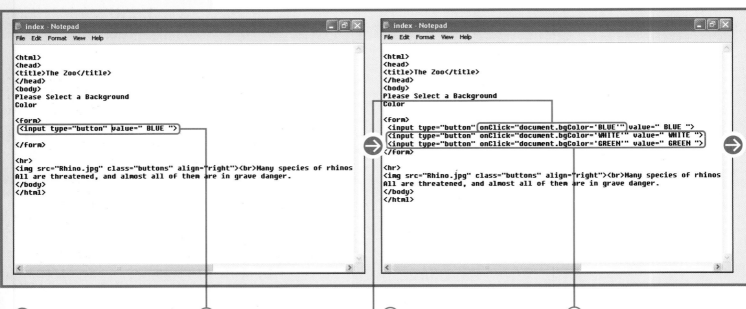

① Open or create a Web page for which you want to allow users to change the background color.

② Type the text that creates a button on the Web page.

③ Type **onClick="document. bgColor='?'"**, replacing ? with the name of a background color.

④ Repeat steps **2** and **3** for each background color you want to let the user choose.

⑤ Save your Web page.

Apply It! ⁂

You can add the onClick
attribute not only to an input button
tag but also to other elements of a
Web page. Doing so enables users to
choose the background by clicking something
other than a button. For example, you can use
the img tag and the a tag to allow users to click
images or links to choose the background.

Did You Know? ⁂

When specifying names for a new
background color, you are not limited to
using simple color names. While you should
use descriptive names on the buttons, you can
also specify an HTML color code as the color
to which you set the background.

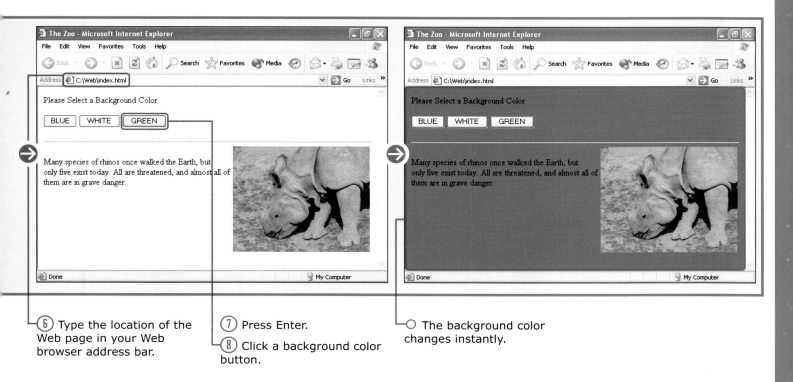

⑥ Type the location of the
Web page in your Web
browser address bar.

⑦ Press Enter.

⑧ Click a background color
button.

○ The background color
changes instantly.

CHAPTER 3

Increase the Effectiveness of Your Links

Links make it possible to combine text, video, and other media to enhance the appearance and interactivity of your Web page. They also allow you to access Web pages from servers all around the world.

When you utilize links, you can create interactive menus and offer more information about the content of your Web site. You can also access diverse Internet services other than just those that simply link to Web pages. You can create links that not only add functionality to your Web pages, but also improve the appearance of the Web page contents.

You create a simple link using the link tag a, or *anchor tag*, with the href attribute, which specifies the name of a Web page to which you want to link. Traditionally, when

users select a link, the page to which you establish the link opens and replaces the current Web page in the Web browser window.

You can represent links with a wide variety of items, including text, buttons, and even images. You must begin the link tag with a start tag, or opening a tag, containing the attributes of the link, such as the Web page to which you want to link. You must place the end tag, or closing tag, after the link item, which is commonly text or an image.

You should make links as short and concise as possible. Regardless of the type of link you use, it should stand out on your Web page so that users can find it quickly and easily. This is why links are commonly underlined.

TOP 100

<td>
<tbody> <thead> <tr>
<table>

Send an
E-MAIL MESSAGE
VIA A LINK

You can add a link to a Web page that enables a user to send you an e-mail message upon activation. Creating an e-mail message link allows you to specify the address of the e-mail message and the subject of the message.

You turn an item into a link by placing a line of JavaScript code in the HTML tag that creates the item. The onClick attribute specifies the JavaScript code that runs when a user clicks the item.

When you assign message details to the JavaScript property location.href, the e-mail program of the user launches and allows them to type a message. For the e-mail link to work, users must have a properly installed and configured e-mail program.

The value of location.href is the keyword mailto, followed by the e-mail address where you want to send the message. You can set the subject of the message by appending a question mark and the keyword subject, followed by the subject of the message.

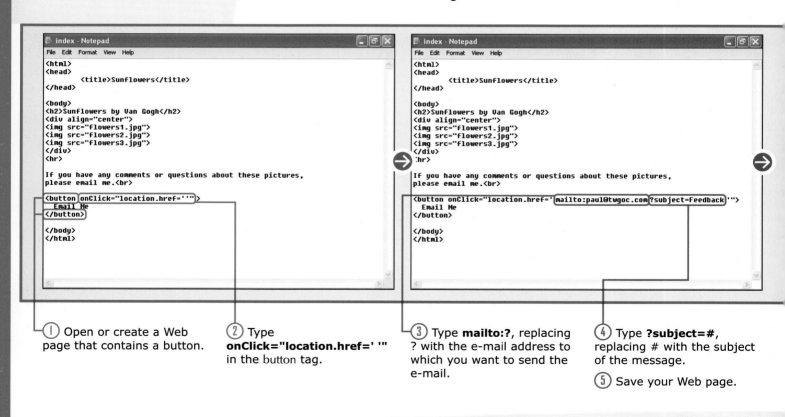

① Open or create a Web page that contains a button.

② Type **onClick="location.href=' '"** in the button tag.

③ Type **mailto:?**, replacing ? with the e-mail address to which you want to send the e-mail.

④ Type **?subject=#**, replacing # with the subject of the message.

⑤ Save your Web page.

Caution! ☀

Whenever you create a link to an e-mail message from a Web page, make sure that the specified e-mail address is current. If you have e-mail links on your Web pages, you must update those links whenever you change your e-mail address.

DIFFICULTY LEVEL

Customize It! ☀

You can create links to e-mail messages using many different items, including text and images. To use an image as a link, simply add the JavaScript code to the img HTML tag. For example:

```
<img src="go.gif"
onClick="location.href='mailto:p@twgoc.com?subject=Hi'">
```

⑥ Type the location of the Web page in your Web browser address bar.

⑦ Press Enter.

⑧ Click the e-mail button.

○ The e-mail program window opens, and a new e-mail message appears with the To and Subject fields complete.

Create an
IMAGE MAP

An image map is an image that you can divide into separate sections, with each section acting as a link to another Web page. When a mouse pointer passes over an area of an image that you use as a link, it changes so that the user knows it is an active link.

To create an image map, you must first obtain an image or create one in an image-editing program. You add image maps to a Web page using the image tag img. You can then add the usemap attribute to the img tag to identify the image map.

A separate map tag sets up the coordinates for the area of the image that you want to become the image map. The map tag contains the name of the image map, along with the area tags that specify the coordinates of the areas of the image that contain links. It also includes the Web pages to which you want to link. The coordinates describe the top-left and the bottom-right corners of each rectangular image area.

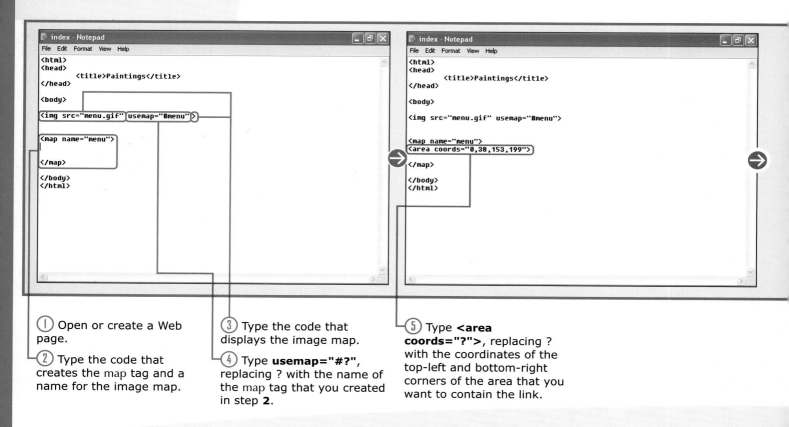

① Open or create a Web page.

② Type the code that creates the map tag and a name for the image map.

③ Type the code that displays the image map.

④ Type **usemap="#?"**, replacing ? with the name of the map tag that you created in step **2**.

⑤ Type **<area coords="?">**, replacing ? with the coordinates of the top-left and bottom-right corners of the area that you want to contain the link.

Caution! ☀

Any image you use should have
very distinct areas, so that users
can tell which parts of the image you
are using as links. Complex images, such
as photographs, can make it very hard for
users to discern link areas. You should make the
majority of your image a link; otherwise, the user
may have to move the mouse pointer all over the
image looking for the link.

Apply It! ☀

Determining the correct coordinates is a matter
of trial and error until the coordinates in the map
tag correspond to the area of the image you want
to use as a link. To save time, you can use an
image-editing program to help determine the
coordinates that you need to use in the map tag.

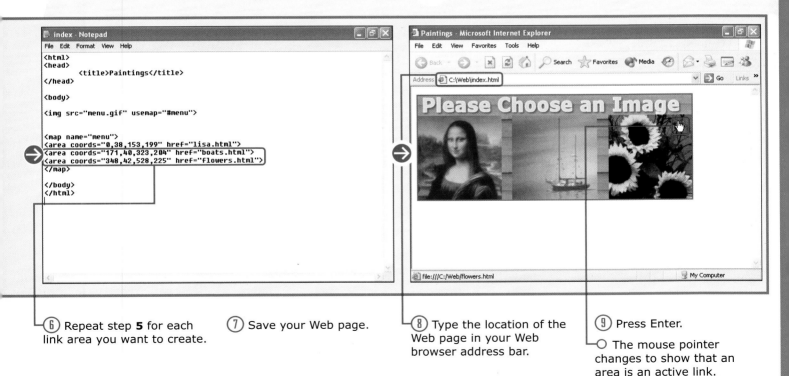

⑥ Repeat step **5** for each
link area you want to create.

⑦ Save your Web page.

⑧ Type the location of the
Web page in your Web
browser address bar.

⑨ Press Enter.

○ The mouse pointer
changes to show that an
area is an active link.

REMOVE UNDERLINES
from links

When you use HTML code to create a text link, the Web browser automatically underlines the text to indicate that the text is a link and not just regular text. You can remove the underline from text links to improve the appearance of your Web page.

You can use the a tag to create a link. You can then apply a style to the a tag by creating a style block in the head section of the HTML code. This allows you to apply specific properties to the a tag. When you

create a style block with the name a, the properties in that style block apply to all links in the Web page. That means that the style applies not only to text links, but also to other links, such as image links.

The property that controls the appearance, including the underline, of a link is the text-decoration property. The text-decoration property can contain a number of values, including none, which removes the underline from the text.

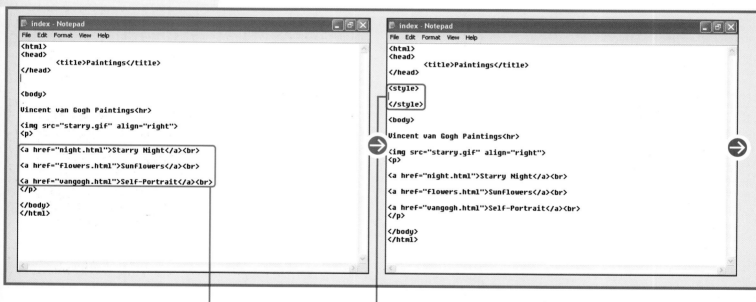

① Open or create a Web page.

② Type the code that creates text links in the Web page.

③ Type the opening and closing style tags.

21

Caution! ☀

Because Web page developers
have underlined text links since
the beginning of the World Wide Web,
most people expect to find them on Web
pages. If you remove your text links'
underlines, make sure that the user can still
recognize them as links. For example, avoid using
a color that makes your text links indistinguishable
from the surrounding text.

Apply It! ☀

As well as remove the underline, you can also
apply a different color to the links to make
them appear more obvious. To change the text
color, specify a color property on the style block
that you create for the a tag:

```
a{
text-decoration : overline;
                color : Black;
}
```

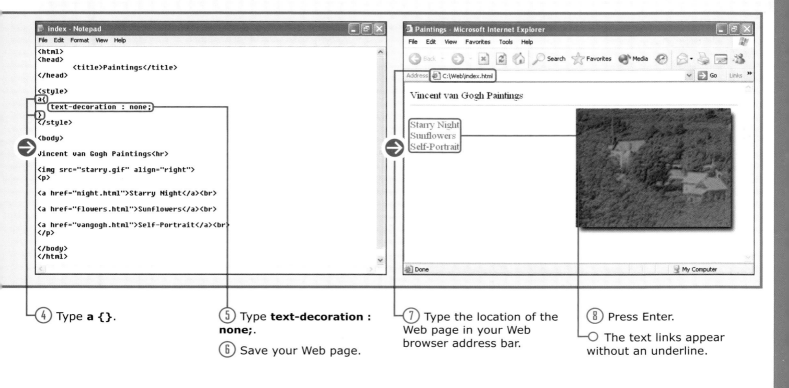

④ Type **a {}**.

⑤ Type **text-decoration :
none;**.

⑥ Save your Web page.

⑦ Type the location of the
Web page in your Web
browser address bar.

⑧ Press Enter.

○ The text links appear
without an underline.

CREATE A LINK TO
download a file

You can create a link that downloads a file to a computer. When a user activates a link to a file, the Web browser should display a number of options to the user. For example, the Web browser typically asks the user where on their computer they want to save the file.

You create a link to a file in the exact same way that you create a link to a Web page, except that instead of specifying a Web page link in the a tag, you

specify the name of a file. The Web page continues to display in the Web browser while you download the file.

Most operating systems are configured to handle different file types in different ways. For example, some operating systems automatically try to run any file that you download if the file ends with the .exe extension. In many cases Web browsers automatically start to download any file to which you link.

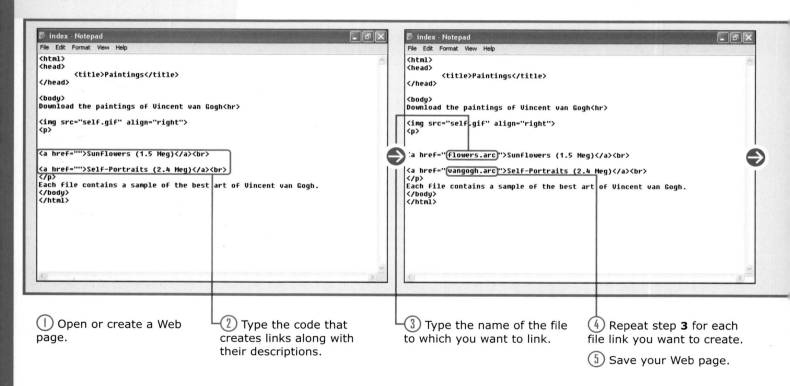

① Open or create a Web page.

② Type the code that creates links along with their descriptions.

③ Type the name of the file to which you want to link.

④ Repeat step **3** for each file link you want to create.

⑤ Save your Web page.

Did You Know? ☀

To make the transfer of
multiple files easier, place them in
a single file called an *archive*. Most
programs can archive and compress files.
Most operating systems have utilities that
can create file archives. Refer to your operating
system documentation for more information.

Caution! ☀

When you make files available on your Web page,
you may want to verify that the users can use the
files. For example, programs that work on
the Windows operating system do not work
correctly on the Mac or Linux operating systems.

id You Know? ☀

When creating a link to a file, you should indicate
the file's size. This helps users to determine how long
it may take for them to download the file.

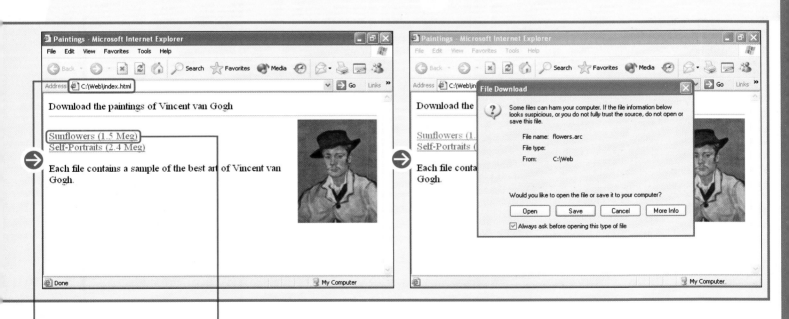

⑥ Type the location of the
Web page in your Web
browser address bar.

⑦ Press Enter.

⑧ Click a link to a file.

○ The Web browser asks
you what you want to do
with the downloaded file.

Access other
INTERNET SERVICES

Most people are familiar with the HTTP protocol, which accesses Web pages. However, you can also create links that use other protocols that provide different services on the Internet or on your own network.

You can identify the protocol you have in use by looking in the address bar of the Web browser. All standard Web pages utilize the prefix of the protocol that the Web browser is using.

One of the more popular protocols is telnet, which accesses the telnet service from your Web browser. Telnet allows you to log onto and communicate with

computers that use a text-based interface. Gopher, which uses the gopher protocol, is an older service similar to the World Wide Web. Likewise, you access secure Web pages using the https protocol.

You can use the a tag to create a link to an Internet service, except that instead of specifying a link to a Web page, you must use the name of a computer prefixed with the protocol that the service uses, for example: gopher://.

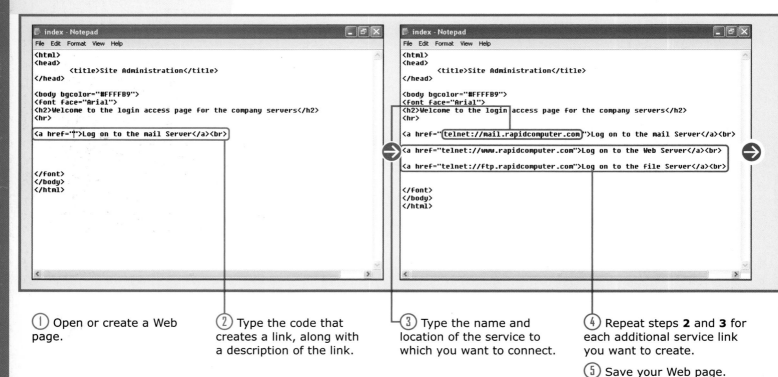

① Open or create a Web page.

② Type the code that creates a link, along with a description of the link.

③ Type the name and location of the service to which you want to connect.

④ Repeat steps **2** and **3** for each additional service link you want to create.

⑤ Save your Web page.

Customize It! ※

When Web browsers encounter a protocol, they load other applications, called *helper applications*, to use the service that the protocol represents. Although most operating systems include basic helper applications, you can install your own, more customized, helper applications. The Web browser runs them automatically when needed.

Did You Know? ※

You can use protocols other than HTTP to access different services on your computer or on the Internet.

Common Web Browser Protocols	
Protocol	*Purpose*
https	Secure Web pages.
gopher	An information system similar to the Web.
ftp	Use to download files.
wais	Use to access a document-cataloging service.
file	Use to access files that you store locally.

#23

DIFFICULTY LEVEL

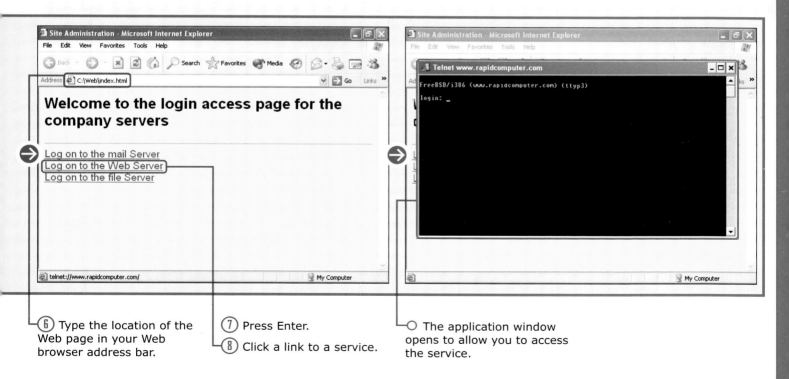

⑥ Type the location of the Web page in your Web browser address bar.

⑦ Press Enter.

⑧ Click a link to a service.

○ The application window opens to allow you to access the service.

Create
LINKS WITHIN LONG DOCUMENTS

If your Web page contains a lot of information, it may extend past the display area of your Web browser window. This means that users must scroll through the Web page in order to see the rest of it. You can create links that take users directly to specific areas on the Web page.

You can use the a tag to name an area of the Web page to which you want to link. This is referred to as a *named anchor*. You create a link that enables

users to access the named anchor on the Web page. The name attribute of the a tag identifies the named anchor. The value of the name attribute then becomes the value of the href attribute, preceded by a hash symbol, #.

Long Web pages typically have a menu at the top of the Web page, which allows users to quickly navigate through the Web page.

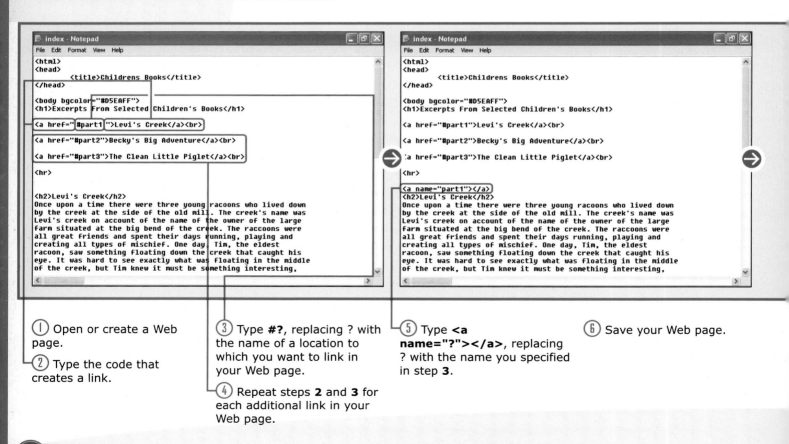

① Open or create a Web page.

② Type the code that creates a link.

③ Type **#?**, replacing ? with the name of a location to which you want to link in your Web page.

④ Repeat steps **2** and **3** for each additional link in your Web page.

⑤ Type **<a name="?"></a>**, replacing ? with the name you specified in step **3**.

⑥ Save your Web page.

#24

DIFFICULTY LEVEL

Caution! ☀

The value you use for the name attribute can only contain numbers and letters. If you include characters such as spacing, the link to that part of the Web page may not work properly.

Apply It! ☀

Not only can you provide links to other locations on your Web page, you can also link from these locations back to the top of the Web page. This makes it easier for users to navigate your Web pages.

Did You Know? ☀

Many people do not like to scroll through long Web pages. This means they do not generally read much of the information on long Web pages. Try to divide your content into several, smaller Web pages.

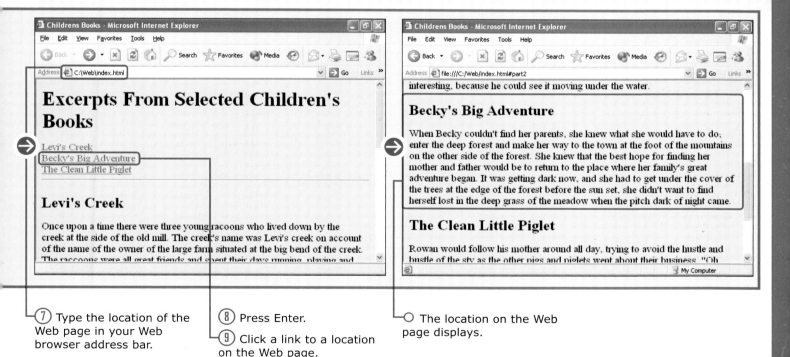

⑦ Type the location of the Web page in your Web browser address bar.

⑧ Press Enter.

⑨ Click a link to a location on the Web page.

○ The location on the Web page displays.

Explain a link with a
LINK TOOL TIP

You can create tool tips to explain to a user where a link on a Web page takes them. Tool tips are small, floating boxes that contain information that is helpful to a user. They appear when a user moves the mouse pointer over a link on a Web page.

Typically, the Web browser displays the address of a link in the status bar at the bottom of the Web browser window when the user moves the mouse pointer over the link. Tool tips can provide more detailed information about the link.

You can add tool tips to links using the title attribute of the a tag. You make the value of the title attribute the descriptive text that explains the purpose of the link.

You should make the descriptive text in a tool tip no longer than a sentence or two. The tool tip only appears for a few seconds, and if you make text too long, the user cannot read the complete tool tip before it disappears.

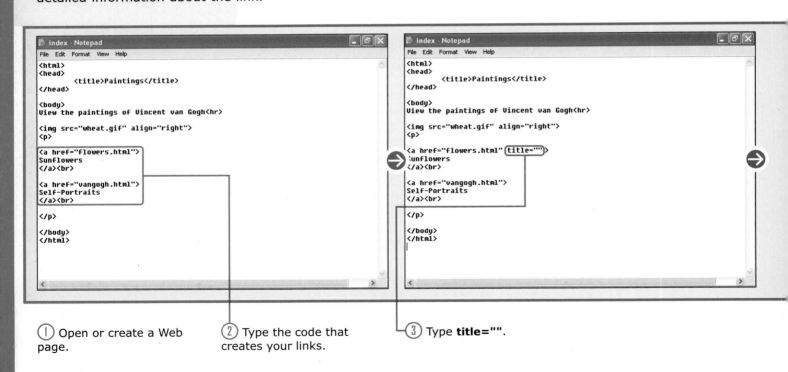

① Open or create a Web page.

② Type the code that creates your links.

③ Type **title=""**.

25

Cross-Platform! ※

The appearance of the tool tip may differ depending on the operating system and the type of Web browser that you are using. For example, on a computer running Windows XP, the tool tip appears in a yellow box, while on a computer running Mac OS, the tool tip may appear in a cartoon-like pop-up balloon.

Apply It! ※

You can also use the alt attribute to provide information about images. Although some Web browsers use the alt attribute information as the text for the tool tip if the title attribute is not present in the a tag, the value of the alt attribute usually appears if an image fails to load. For example:

<a href="cars.html" alt="information about our car collection">Cars</a>

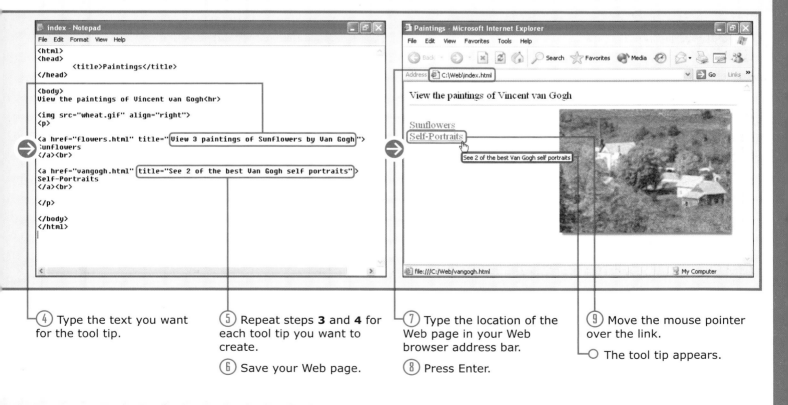

④ Type the text you want for the tool tip.

⑤ Repeat steps **3** and **4** for each tool tip you want to create.

⑥ Save your Web page.

⑦ Type the location of the Web page in your Web browser address bar.

⑧ Press Enter.

⑨ Move the mouse pointer over the link.

○ The tool tip appears.

Create
DYNAMIC LINK TEXT

You can cause the appearance of your link text to change when a user moves a mouse pointer over it. Changing the behavior of the link in this manner can make your Web page more interesting. It also lets users know when they are encountering links on your Web page.

To change the behavior of link text, you can place a style block with the name a:hover in the head section of the HTML code. This style block allows you to apply different styles to the link text when the mouse pointer hovers, or moves over, the link.

You can specify the styles you want to apply to the link using style properties. The font-weight property with a value of bold changes the text from normal to bold type. The color property lets you set the color of the link text, while the font-style property makes the text italic.

Any style information that you specify in a style block applies to all links on the same page.

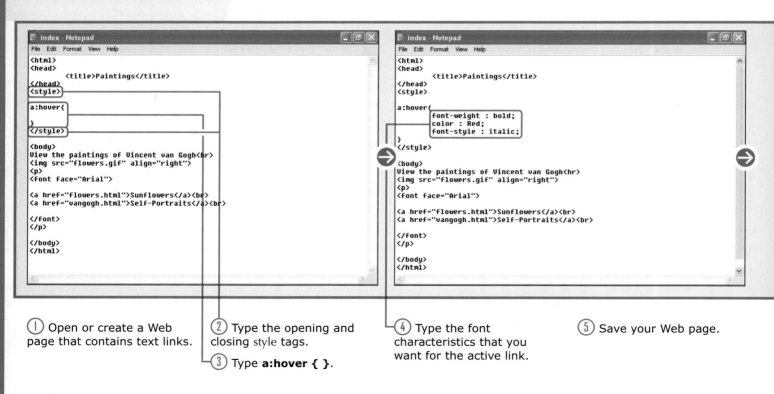

① Open or create a Web page that contains text links.

② Type the opening and closing style tags.

③ Type **a:hover { }**.

④ Type the font characteristics that you want for the active link.

⑤ Save your Web page.

Apply It! ※

You can apply formatting to links that a user has not yet visited. You do this by creating a style block called a:link. The style applies to all links on the Web page, not just the link over which you move the mouse pointer:

```
a:link {
        font-weight : bold;
    color : blue;
font-style : italic;
        }
```

Apply It! ※

Applying a style is not the only way to show an active link. Using the border property, you can also place a border around the link:

```
a:hover {
        border : solid;
    }
```

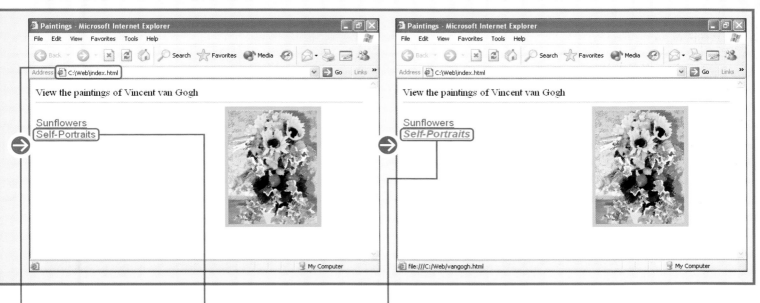

⑥ Type the location of the Web page in your Web browser address bar.

⑦ Press Enter.

⑧ Move the mouse pointer over the link.

○ The appearance of the link text changes.

Using a link to
OPEN A NEW WINDOW

When users select a link, the link typically opens in the same Web browser window, replacing the Web page that contained the link. However, you can instruct a link to open the new page in a new Web browser window. Your Web page can instruct a Web browser to open a new window so that users do not have to leave your Web site when they select links to other Web pages.

Opening pages in new windows is useful if you plan to include links to other Web sites on your Web

pages. This is because users can still see the content of the other Web sites, but your Web site remains accessible in another Web browser window.

The target attribute of the link tag a, specifies the name of a Web browser window. If the name you specify is _blank, then the Web page to which you are linking opens and appears in a new Web browser window.

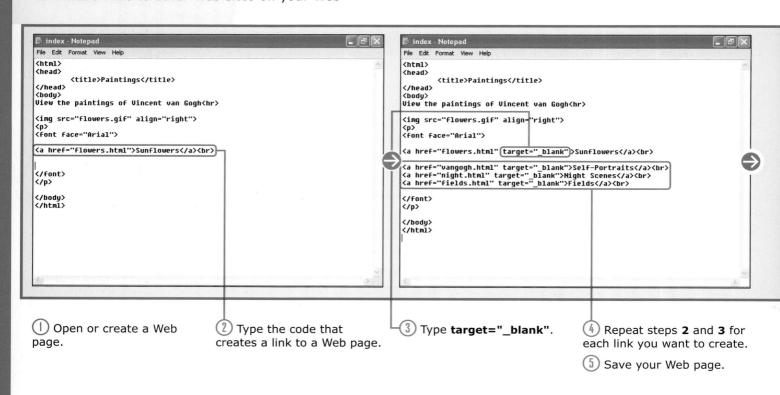

① Open or create a Web page.

② Type the code that creates a link to a Web page.

③ Type **target="_blank"**.

④ Repeat steps **2** and **3** for each link you want to create.

⑤ Save your Web page.

#27

DIFFICULTY LEVEL

Caution! ☀

When specifying the target attribute value, do not omit the underscore character, _ , before the word blank.

Apply It ☀

You can use the _self target value to instruct the Web browser to load the Web page link in the same window as your Web page:

`<a href="fields.html" target="_self">Fields</a>`

Apply It ☀

If you use a value other than _blank for the target attribute, the Web page still opens in a new window. When the user activates subsequent links, however, the Web pages do not open new Web browser windows. Instead the links open in the window created when the user activated the first link.

`<a href="fields.html" target="window">Fields</a>`

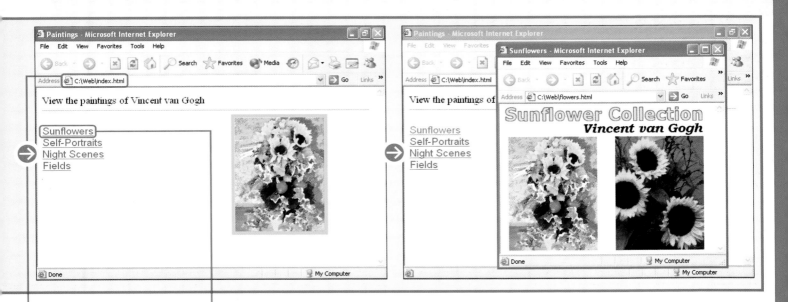

⑥ Type the location of the Web page in your Web browser address bar.

⑦ Press Enter.

⑧ Click a link.

○ The Web page opens in a new window.

CHAPTER 4

Jazz Up Your Site with Multimedia

Multimedia in Web pages generally refers to items such as images, video, audio, and animations that you can add to a Web page. Multimedia items help to make the appearance of Web pages more pleasing as well as provide a means of conveying information. Instead of pages of text instruction on how to accomplish a task, you can now add a video to your Web page to demonstrate how to perform the task.

In the past, Web browsers had difficulty playing multimedia in a Web page and they forced the user to separately download multimedia items and access them using programs other than a Web browser.

It was not that long ago that the processing speed of computers and the low connection speeds made it almost impossible to provide usable multimedia-enabled Web pages. Fortunately, most computers can now access a wide range of multimedia content. With the increase in the number of users accessing Web pages with networks or high speed Internet connections, you can now use sophisticated multimedia elements directly in a Web page.

Today's Web browsers and HTML code have made it much easier to provide multimedia content, even video, right in a Web page. While Web browsers still do not completely agree in the way multimedia content should be provided in a Web page, most users can access any multimedia content that you want to add to your Web pages.

TOP 100

Display images from
ANOTHER WEB SITE

You can display images stored on another computer within a Web page, which you have created and stored on your own computer or on another Web server. You may want to display images from another Web server for a variety of reasons. For example, you can display a company logo on each Web page without creating multiple copies of the logo image.

You can use the HTML image tag img, the same standard image tag that displays images located on your computer, to display images in a Web page.

The src attribute of the image tag specifies the name of the image that displays. The difference is that when you specify the image name using the src attribute, you specify the Web address of the image.

When you frequently change images, the image filenames also change. For example, each image displaying information about the weather may use a different name, one for every day of the week. This means that the filename for today may differ from the filename for tomorrow, and this may prevent your image from displaying on your page.

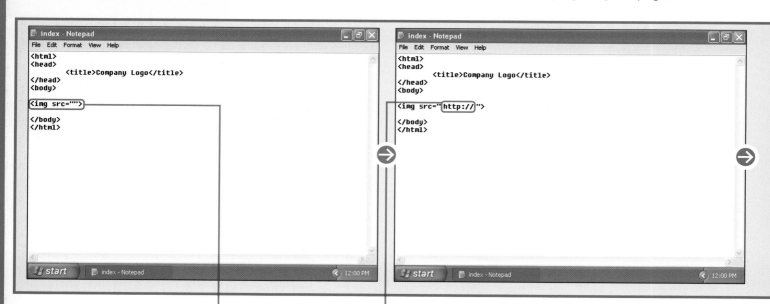

① Open or create an HTML page in a text editor.

② Type **<img *src*="">** where you want the image to display, replacing *src* with the attribute that specifies the address of the image.

○ This creates an empty value.

③ Position the cursor between the quotes and type the value **http://**.

DIFFICULTY LEVEL

Caution!

When you link to an image
stored on another Web site, the
Web site must transfer the image each
time your Web page displays. This
requires the Web server that stores the image
to use some of its available resources, such as
processing power and connection bandwidth,
to make the image available to your Web page.
When using images from another Web server,
you should inform, and get permission from,
the owner of that Web server.

Did You Know?

In most countries, including the U.S., there
are specific laws that forbid the use of images,
in any media such as the Web or a book,
without first securing permission from the owner
of the image.

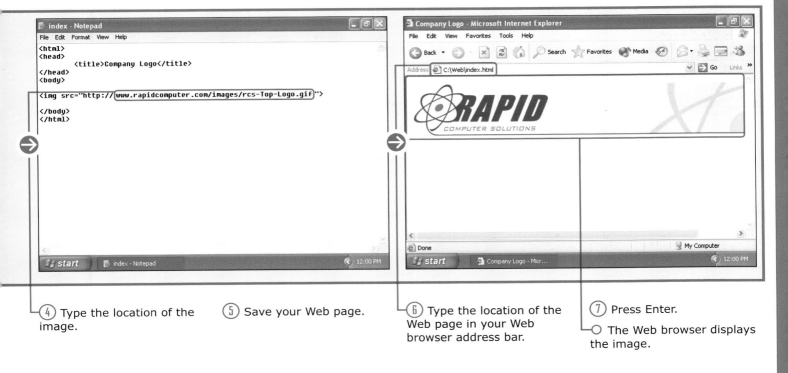

4 Type the location of the image.

5 Save your Web page.

6 Type the location of the Web page in your Web browser address bar.

7 Press Enter.

○ The Web browser displays the image.

Using spacer images to PRECISELY POSITION GRAPHICS

Web page creation can become frustrating when you cannot precisely align images on your Web page. This causes the same Web page to appear differently when users view it on different Web browsers and different monitors. You can use a small spacer image to help align graphics on a Web page so that the Web page looks more consistent. If the spacer image is the same color as the Web page background, it appears invisible on the Web page.

You can create a spacer image using an image-editing program. You should make the image quite

small, even as small as one pixel wide by one pixel high.

You can control the size at which a spacer image displays on a Web page. You do this by manipulating the width and height attributes of the img tag that specifies the spacer image.

To ensure that users do not see the spacer image on the Web page, you can specify the border of the image as zero. This prevents a Web browser from drawing a border around the spacer image.

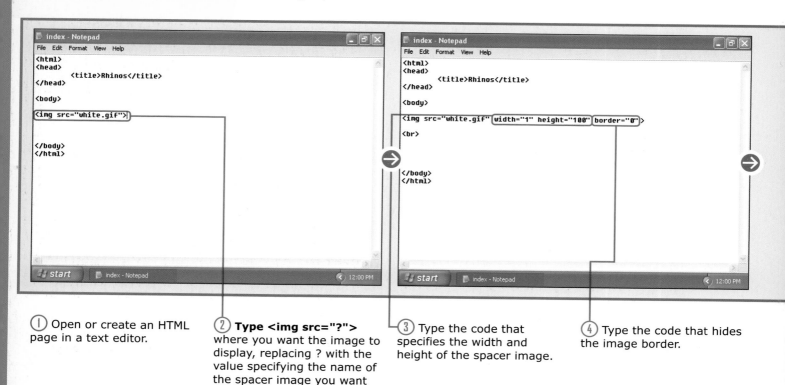

① Open or create an HTML page in a text editor.

② **Type <img src="?">** where you want the image to display, replacing ? with the value specifying the name of the spacer image you want to use.

③ Type the code that specifies the width and height of the spacer image.

④ Type the code that hides the image border.

DIFFICULTY LEVEL

Customize It!

When you create a small image to use as the spacer image, ensure that it does not stand out from the Web page background. Many image-editing programs allow you to create transparent images that appear invisible when you view them on a Web page. Creating a transparent spacer image allows you to use any image as the Web page background.

Apply It!

You can also use spacer images to help position other Web page elements, such as text paragraphs and horizontal rules.

Did You Know?

You can set up and align your spacer images by drawing a border around them. To do this, simply change the border size to 1:

<img src="white.gif" width="1"height="100" border="1">

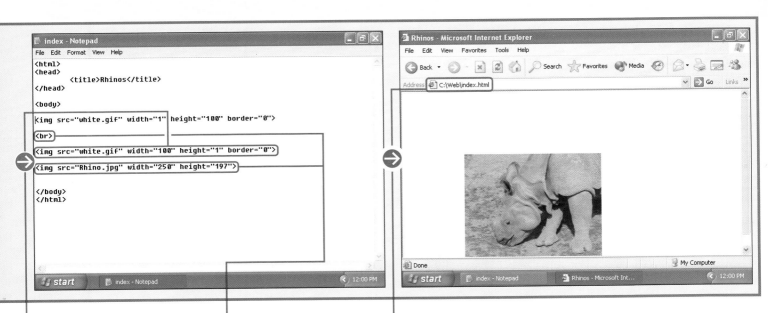

(5) Repeat steps **2** to **4** for each spacer image you want to use.

(6) Type the content of your Web page.

(7) Save your Web page.

(8) Type the location of the Web page in your Web browser address bar.

(9) Press Enter.

○ The Web page displays.

You can change the size at which an image displays in a Web page without having to resize the original image using an image-editing program. The img tag has attributes that you use to specify the dimensions of the image as it displays on the Web page, regardless of the actual size of the image.

The height attribute of the img tag defines the height at which the image displays, while the width attribute specifies the width at which it displays. The values of the height and width attributes specify the height and width, in pixels, at which you want the

image to appear. As with all HTML attribute values, you should enclose the values of the height and width attributes in quotes.

You can use the img tag multiple times in the same Web page to display the same image, even at different dimensions. When you omit the size attributes of the img tag, the Web browser displays the image at the actual size of the image.

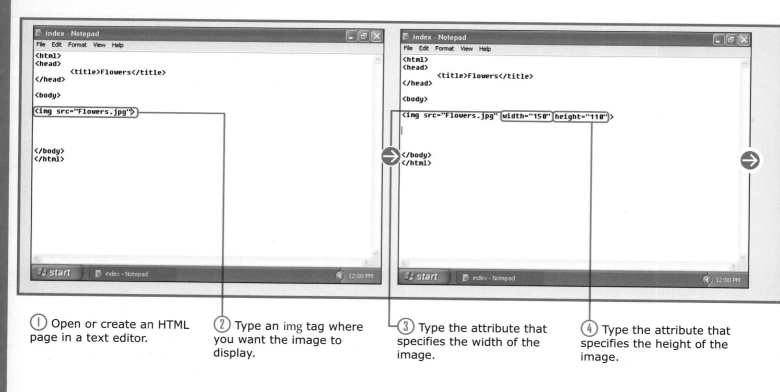

① Open or create an HTML page in a text editor.

② Type an img tag where you want the image to display.

③ Type the attribute that specifies the width of the image.

④ Type the attribute that specifies the height of the image.

DIFFICULTY LEVEL

Caution!

You can easily resize an image so that the image that displays is larger than the actual size of the original image. Keep in mind that when you display an image at greater than the original size, the quality of the image deteriorates. This is particularly true for images that contain a lot of detail, such as images of photographs.

Did You Know?

The size of the image as it displays in a browser window depends on the resolution of the user's display. An image that displays with a width of 500 pixels looks quite large when you view it on a display with a resolution of 640 by 480 pixels, but it barely stretches halfway across a display that has a resolution of 1024 by 768 pixels.

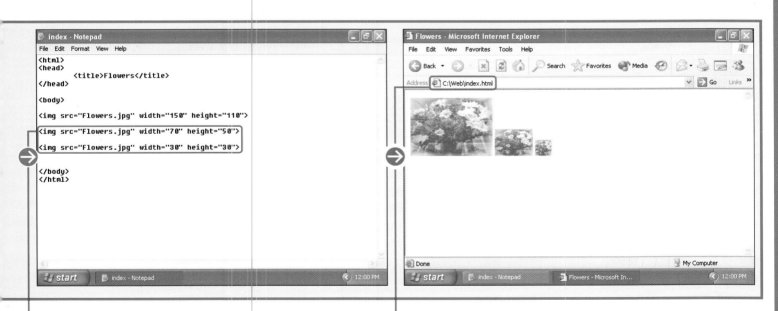

⑤ Repeat steps **2** to **4** for each placement of the image, using different values each time for the width and height attributes.

⑥ Save your Web page.

⑦ Type the location of the Web page in your Web browser address bar.

⑧ Press Enter.

○ The Web browser displays the image at different sizes.

Preload an image to increase
Preload an image to increase
DISPLAY SPEED

You can preload images into a Web page to increase the speed at which the Web page displays. Each time an image displays in a Web page, the Web browser must wait while the image transfers from the Web server before the Web browser can display the image and the remainder of the Web page. By preloading images, you ensure that all the images transfer before the Web page displays.

You can preload images by inserting JavaScript code within the head section of the HTML code. The JavaScript code creates a new image object at

dimensions you specify for each image, and then you simply specify the name of the image file you want to use.

Although you use JavaScript to preload the image, the image displays using the HTML img tag. All the JavaScript code does is instruct your Web browser to transfer the image to your computer so that when the image displays, the Web browser retrieves it from the cache of files on your computer instead of the Web server.

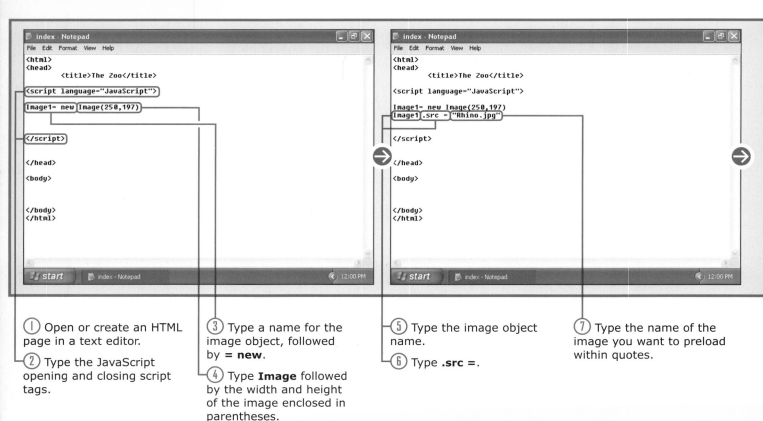

① Open or create an HTML page in a text editor.

② Type the JavaScript opening and closing script tags.

③ Type a name for the image object, followed by **= new**.

④ Type **Image** followed by the width and height of the image enclosed in parentheses.

⑤ Type the image object name.

⑥ Type **.src =**.

⑦ Type the name of the image you want to preload within quotes.

DIFFICULTY LEVEL

Did You Know? ❊

You do not have to use preloaded images in the Web page that causes the images to preload. You can access preloaded images from other Web pages on your Web site without having to load the images again. For example, you can preload images that you use in other areas of your Web site on your Home page. While the time to load the home page may be longer, all the other Web pages load faster because you preloaded the images.

Apply It! ❊

You do not usually need to preload images on a typical Web page. However, preloading images makes a dramatic difference when you use them with other special effects, such as image rollovers. For information on how to create image rollovers, see task #84.

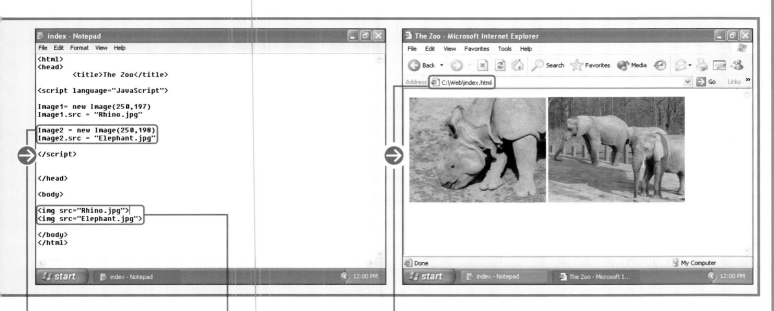

⑧ Repeat steps **3** to **7** for each image you want to preload.

⑨ Type the code that displays the preloaded images.

⑩ Save your Web page.

⑪ Type the location of the Web page in your Web browser address bar.

⑫ Press Enter.

○ The Web browser displays the preloaded images.

79

Preload a
LOW-RESOLUTION IMAGE

You can display a smaller version of a much larger image in a browser prior to displaying the larger image. Displaying a smaller version of an image allows the user to preview the image without having to wait for the image to load completely.

You need two versions of an image in order to use the lowsrc attribute. The first version of the image is the normal image that displays in the Web page. The second version is smaller than the normal image. The smaller image is typically a lower resolution or black-and-white version of the normal image.

You specify the name of the preloaded image using the lowsrc attribute of the image tag. When you type the code that preloads a low-resolution image, you should always specify the width and height of the image.

Not all Web browsers support the lowsrc attribute, however, the popular Netscape Navigator browser does. Netscape Navigator is available at www.netscape.com.

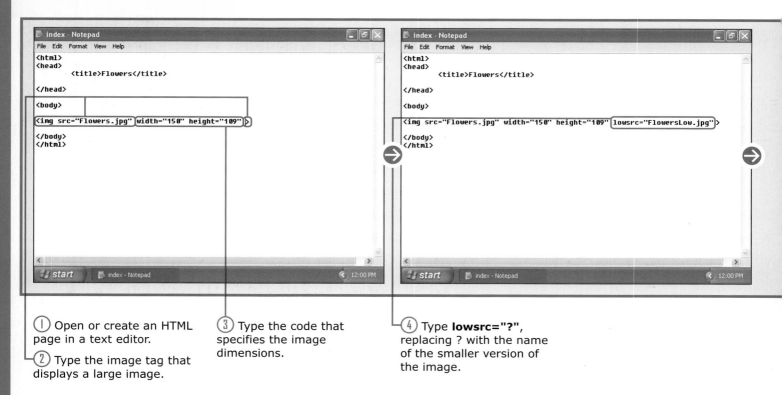

① Open or create an HTML page in a text editor.

② Type the image tag that displays a large image.

③ Type the code that specifies the image dimensions.

④ Type **lowsrc="?"**, replacing ? with the name of the smaller version of the image.

Cross-Platform!

Not all Web browsers support the lowsrc attribute of the img tag. Netscape Navigator is the most popular Web browser that currently supports the lowsrc attribute. If you use the lowsrc attribute in a Web page and then display it using a Web browser that does not support the lowsrc attribute, the browser ignores the low-resolution image and displays only the regular image.

Apply It!

Preloading a low-resolution image is very effective when you use it with an image map. This is because low-resolution images allow a user to load the image map without waiting for the high-resolution, final image to load.

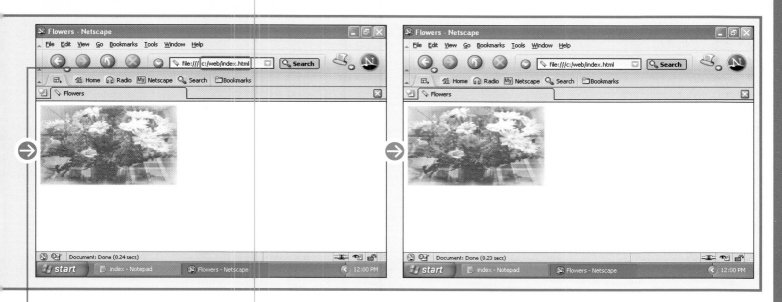

⑤ Type the location of the Web page in your Web browser address bar.

○ This example uses the Netscape Navigator Web browser.

⑥ Press Enter.

○ The Web browser displays the small image.

○ The Web browser then displays the final image.

Using an
IMAGE AS A RULE

You can use an image as a rule on a Web page instead of the plain horizontal rule that you create using the hr tag. You use rules on a Web page to separate different items, such as images and text, or to simply alter the look of the Web page to suit your needs.

One of the features of the hr tag is that you can specify the width of the rule as a percentage of the width between the left and right margins. This allows you to create rules that differ in size depending upon the size of the Web browser window.

If you create or acquire an image that is short and wide, you can use the image as a horizontal rule.

You can also use the width attribute of the img tag to specify the width of the rule as a percentage of the width of the Web browser window. When using an image as a rule, you have the same control over the rule width as you have when you use the HTML hr tag.

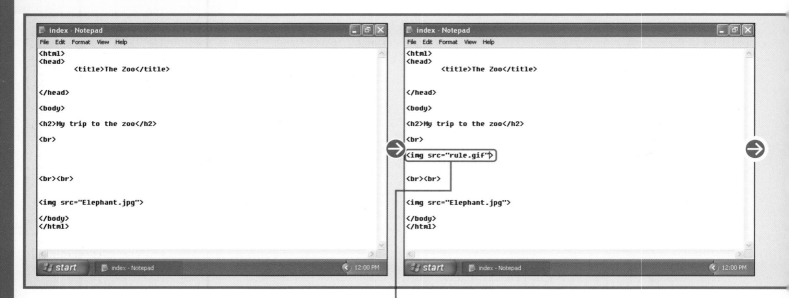

① Open or create an HTML page in a text editor.

② Type the code that displays the image you want to use as a rule.

DIFFICULTY LEVEL

Did You Know?

When you repeatedly use the same image as a horizontal rule throughout a Web page, the image only needs to transfer once to the computer of the user. This makes the loading of Web pages that use the image faster.

Caution!

If you use a complex image as your rule, such as a photographic image, the image may distort as you resize the rule. It is best to use images that consist of solid colors.

Did You Know?

Most operating systems come with their own image-editing programs that allow you to create your own images, which you can then use as horizontal rules. Images that you create yourself should use the .gif file format.

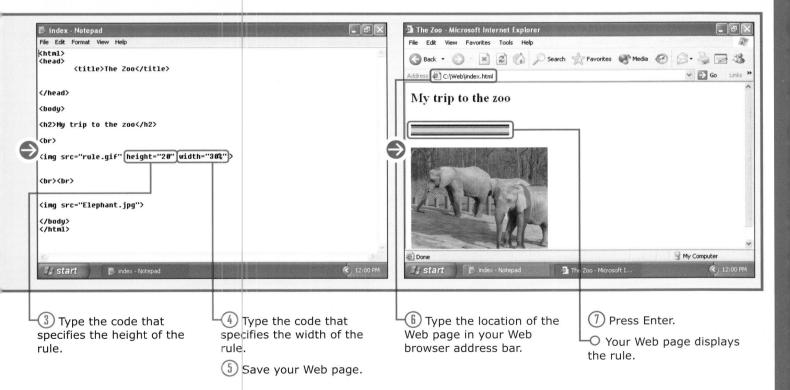

③ Type the code that specifies the height of the rule.

④ Type the code that specifies the width of the rule.

⑤ Save your Web page.

⑥ Type the location of the Web page in your Web browser address bar.

⑦ Press Enter.

○ Your Web page displays the rule.

TEXT WRAPPING AROUND AN IMAGE

You can integrate images and text together on a Web page and make the text flow, or wrap, around multiple images. Controlling the text wrap makes your Web page easier to read and makes the Web page look more aesthetically pleasing.

You can flow text around an image using the align attribute of the image tag. If you do not use the align attribute, only one line of text appears beside the image. You can make the value of the align attribute left or right, depending on where you want to place

the image within the text. Regardless of the align value, you must place the img tag before the text you want to flow around the image.

The best way to use multiple paragraphs with text and images is to use the break tag, br, with the clear attribute to reset the alignment between each paragraph.

When preceding text aligns to the right, the right value of the clear attribute resets the alignment of subsequent text to the default alignment.

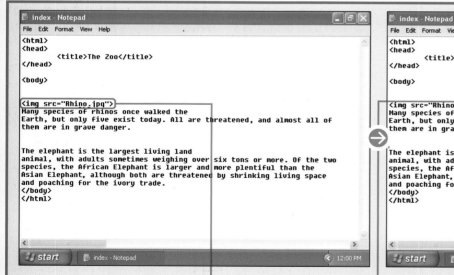

① Open or create an HTML page in a text editor.

② Type the code that inserts an image into the text.

③ Type the code that aligns the image within the text.

Caution!

When users view Web pages that contain text, they can change the size of the text to suit their own preferences. A typical Web browser can display text in a number of sizes from very small to very large. When setting up your Web page, test your Web page's appearance with a variety of text sizes to ensure that they produce the desired results.

DIFFICULTY LEVEL

Apply It!

The clear attribute of the br tag can take one of three values, depending upon the alignment that the preceding section on the Web page uses. Refer to the following table for the appropriate br statement:

br Statement	Usage
<br clear=""left"">	Use after a left aligned item.
<br clear=""right"">	Use after a right aligned item.
<br clear=""all""v>	Use after an item that is left or right aligned.

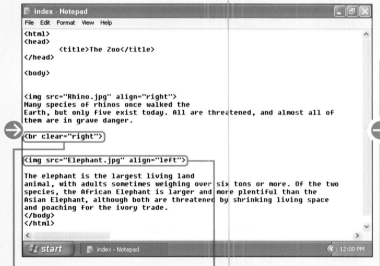

④ Type **<br?>**, replacing ? with the code that resets the margin after the break tag.

⑤ Type the code that displays an image after the break.

⑥ Save your Web page.

⑦ Type the location of the Web page in your Web browser address bar.

⑧ Press Enter.

○ The images align to either side of the page, and the text wraps around them.

QUICK THUMBNAILS

You can create a thumbnail image to allow users to see a preview of a larger image. Users can then view the larger image by clicking the thumbnail image.

You normally create a separate thumbnail image by using an image-editing program to reduce the dimensions of the original image. However, to skip this step and quickly create a thumbnail image in your Web page, you can simply specify a smaller size for the image using the height and width

attributes of the img tag. This allows you to use thumbnails without having to create more images in an image-editing program.

You can use a thumbnail image as a link by enclosing it in the a tag. You can link to a separate Web page that contains the larger image, or you can simply link to the image file itself. When linking to the image file, the Web browser displays the full-sized image. If you want to return to the Web page containing the thumbnail image, you can use the back button in the Web browser.

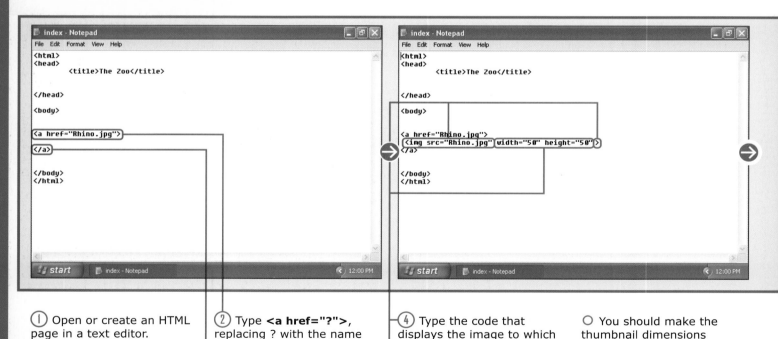

① Open or create an HTML page in a text editor.

② Type **<a href="?">**, replacing ? with the name of an image.

③ Type the closing tag of the a tag that you create in step **2**.

④ Type the code that displays the image to which you link in steps **2** and **3**.

⑤ Type the code that specifies the dimensions of the thumbnail image.

○ You should make the thumbnail dimensions smaller than those of the original image.

⑥ Save your Web page.

Apply It!

By default, a border appears around your thumbnail image to show that the user has previously visited the link. If you do not want to display a border around a thumbnail, set the border attribute of the img tag to 0. For example:

`<img src="Rhino.jpg" width="50" height="50" border="0">`

Caution!

Although the thumbnail appears smaller, the complete image file transfers to the Web browser of the user. This transfer may take a while for large image files. If possible, you should use an image-editing program to produce correctly sized thumbnail images. This ensures that the user does not have to spend an excessive amount of time waiting for what appears to be a small image load.

DIFFICULTY LEVEL

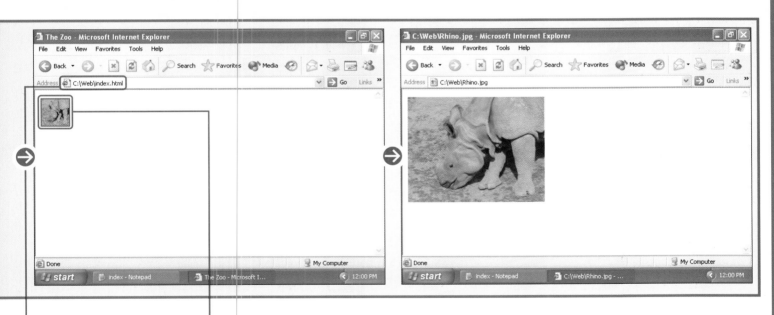

⑦ Type the location of the Web page in your Web browser address bar.

⑧ Press Enter.

○ The thumbnail image displays.

⑨ Click the thumbnail image.

○ The full-size image displays.

Speed a Web page's display by
REUSING IMAGES

You can reuse images throughout your Web site to speed up the display of your Web pages in the Web browser of a user. Reusing the same image throughout your Web site gives the Web pages of your Web site a consistent appearance, and can make your Web site easier to update.

Once a Web browser displays an image, the local computer stores it in a location known as the *cache*. When the Web browser needs to display the same

image again, it retrieves the image from the cache instead of re-transferring the image from the Web server.

Not only can you reuse images throughout a Web page, but you can also reuse them throughout a Web site. You can reuse images as Web page backgrounds and links, as well as simply displaying them on a Web page. Not only can you reuse images in different elements, but you can also change the display size of the images that you are reusing.

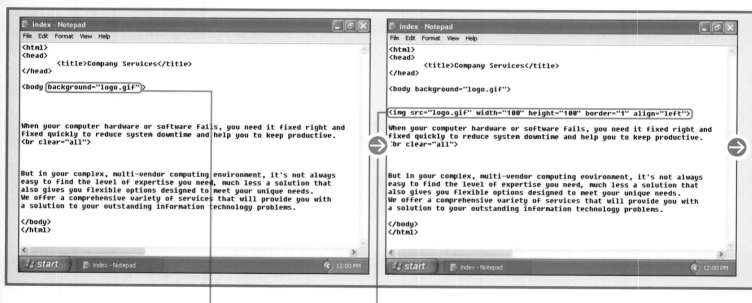

① Open or create an HTML page in a text editor.

② Type the code that displays an image as the Web page background.

③ Type the code that uses the background image from step **2** and displays it as a regular image.

DIFFICULTY LEVEL

Apply It! ☀

Images that are particularly good for reusing are those that make up navigation menus, company logos, and horizontal rules.

Caution! ☀

To reuse an image throughout your Web pages or Web site, you must ensure that the filename for the image is identical each time you use it. In many cases, you might have images that use the same filename, but are located in different directories on the Web server. As well as ensuring that your image files are well organized into directories, you should also pay attention to the use of upper and lower case in the filenames. Web server filenames are almost always case sensitive, so Logo.gif is a different file from logo.gif.

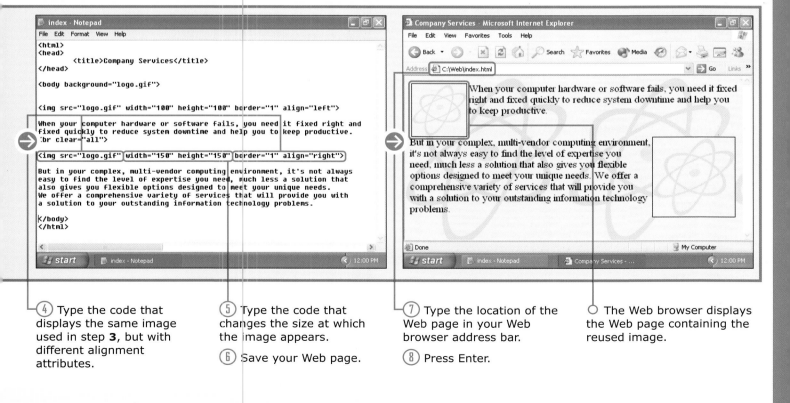

④ Type the code that displays the same image used in step **3**, but with different alignment attributes.

⑤ Type the code that changes the size at which the image appears.

⑥ Save your Web page.

⑦ Type the location of the Web page in your Web browser address bar.

⑧ Press Enter.

○ The Web browser displays the Web page containing the reused image.

LEFT-ALIGN MULTIPLE IMAGES
in a Web page

You can align multiple images to better control the appearance of your Web page.

There is no HTML code that specifically allows you to precisely align images in your Web page. However, you can insert Style Sheet code into an HTML image tag to better control the position of the image. Style Sheet code gives you better control over the placement of elements on a Web page.

The style attribute allows you to place an image an exact distance from the left margin of the Web page. If you use the same distance for all the images on your Web page, they align with each other on their left side. You specify the distance from the left margin in pixels.

The value for the style attribute is margin-left: followed by the number of pixels from the left margin where you want to place the image.

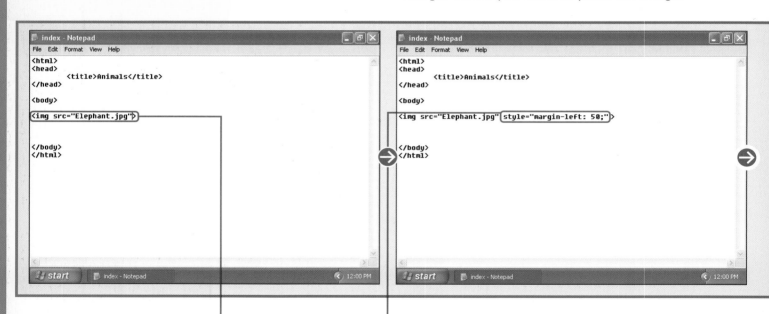

① Open or create an HTML page in a text editor.

② Type the code that displays an image.

③ Type **style="margin-left: ?;"**, replacing ? with the distance from the left margin you want to place the image.

Apply It!

You can use millimeters instead of pixels to specify the distance from the margin to an image. Simply append **mm** to the distance number. The exact distance is not precise because the Web browser has no way of knowing the size of the display on which the user is viewing the Web page. For example:

style="margin-left: 50mm;"

Did You Know?

Using the style attribute to specify a distance from the margin does not have any effect on any other img tag attributes that you specify, such as the align attribute.

Caution!

When you align images, test the appearance of the Web page at different resolutions. Images that align perfectly on displays with higher resolutions may appear incorrectly on very low-resolution displays.

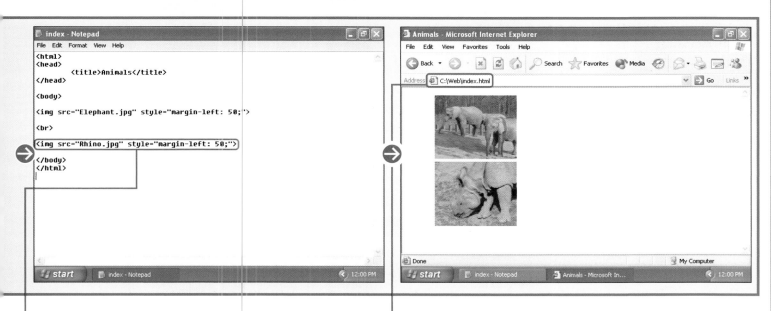

④ Repeat steps **2** and **3** for each image you want to display.

⑤ Save your Web page.

⑥ Type the location of the Web page in your Web browser address bar.

⑦ Press Enter.

○ The images display with a left alignment.

Create an
IMAGE BUTTON

To add flare to your Web page, you can use image buttons instead of the plain button that Web browsers automatically create.

You generally use buttons with forms on a Web page to allow a user to submit data or to start an e-mail program in preparation for creating an e-mail message.

You specify buttons using the input tag. In most forms, you set the type attribute of the input tag to a value of Submit to create a button. To use an image

as a button, you set the value of the type attribute to image and then use an additional attribute, src, to specify the name of the image file you want to use as a button.

You can easily create a simple button using any image-editing program. If the text on the Web page does not explain what the button does, you should ensure that the image on the button explains the purpose of the button.

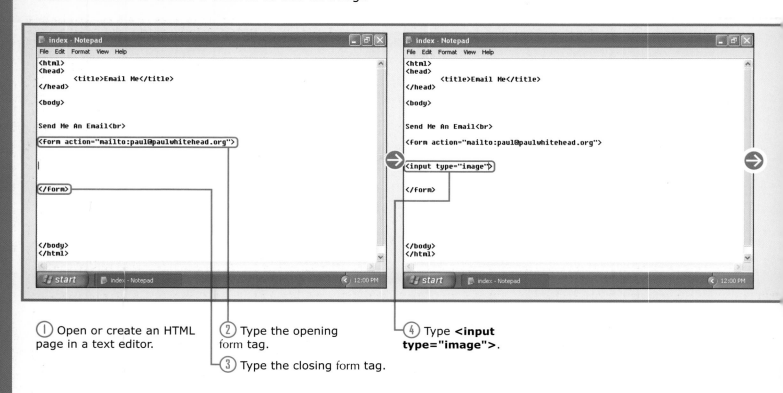

(1) Open or create an HTML page in a text editor.

(2) Type the opening form tag.

(3) Type the closing form tag.

(4) Type **<input type="image">**.

Put It Together! ☀

You can use images as buttons on any form and you do not have to make them pictures or any other type of artwork. Many images that you use as buttons for forms consist of only text formatted with a different appearance. For example, you can use shadows or multi-colored characters, which you cannot possibly create using HTML code.

Apply It! ☀

As with other images, you can align the image button in relation to other items on your Web page. For example, to align the image button to the right margin, use the align attribute with a value of right. For example:

<input type="image" src="button.gif" align="right">

DIFFICULTY LEVEL

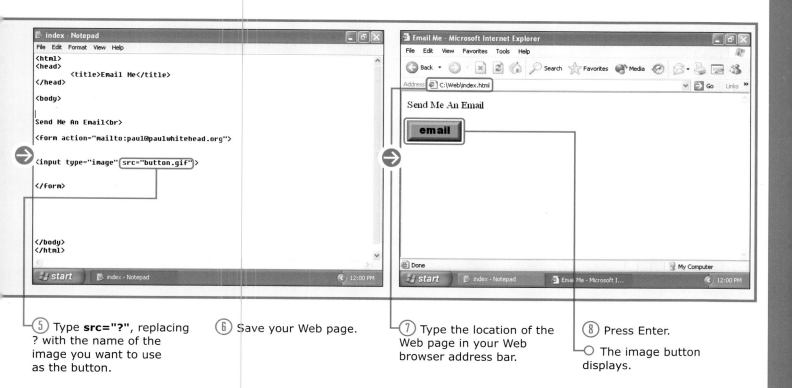

⑤ Type **src="?"**, replacing ? with the name of the image you want to use as the button.

⑥ Save your Web page.

⑦ Type the location of the Web page in your Web browser address bar.

⑧ Press Enter.

○ The image button displays.

Add a
BACKGROUND SOUND
to a Web page

You can add a background sound to your Web page so that it plays a sound when a user views the Web page.

You can use a simple message, such as a welcome message, or a complete song to make your Web page background sounds. You can use sound files in the .wav or .mid format that you can create or acquire from the Internet.

The bgsound tag specifies the name of the sound file that you want to play. Although not all Web browsers support the bgsound tag, Internet Explorer, the most

popular Web browser, does. You must place the bgsound tag within the head section of the HTML code of the Web page.

The bgsound tag specifies the sound filename using the src attribute. You can replay the sound a number of times using the loop attribute.

When users load the Web page, the background sound transfers to their computers. For this reason, you should keep the size of the sound file as small as possible, at most, no more than 200 kilobytes.

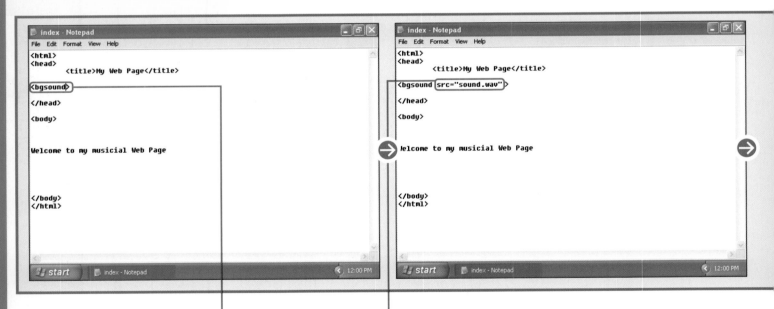

① Open or create an HTML page in a text editor.

② Type **<bgsound>** within the head section of the HTML code.

③ Type **src="?"**, replacing ? with the name of the sound file you want to play.

#39

Caution!

Your sound files are only audible to users who are viewing your Web page on a computer with a working sound system and with the speakers or headphones connected and working. For this reason, you should ensure that any important message in your audio file is also available to users who do not have sound capabilities. You may consider placing a statement somewhere on your Web page that alerts the user to the fact that you have audio information available.

Caution!

Users who view your Web page in a quiet environment, such as an office or a library, may consider background sounds annoying. While background sounds on your personal Web page are acceptable, background sounds are inappropriate on a business site.

DIFFICULTY LEVEL

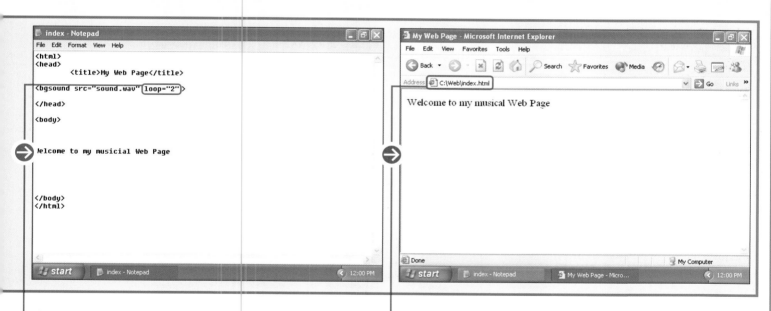

④ Type **loop="?"**, replacing ? with the number of times you want the audio file to play.

⑤ Save your Web page.

⑥ Type the location of the Web page in your Web browser address bar.

⑦ Press Enter.

○ The Web page appears, and the audio file plays.

Add a
MEDIA PLAYER
to play audio files

You can place audio playback controls in your Web page to allow your users to play audio files when they want. This gives your users better control over what audio files they want to play.

You can include the media player in your Web page along with other Web page elements such as images and text. The embed tag can point to a sound file, typically in the .wav file format, to which the user can listen. The user has access to and can select all of the controls usually associated with a media player, such as pause, rewind, and volume control.

You can use the src attribute of the embed tag to indicate the name of the audio file. The embed tag also has width and height attributes that allow you to choose the size at which the media player controls display in your Web page.

If you want audio to start playing when using the media player controls, you can add a background sound to your Web page. For more information, see task #39.

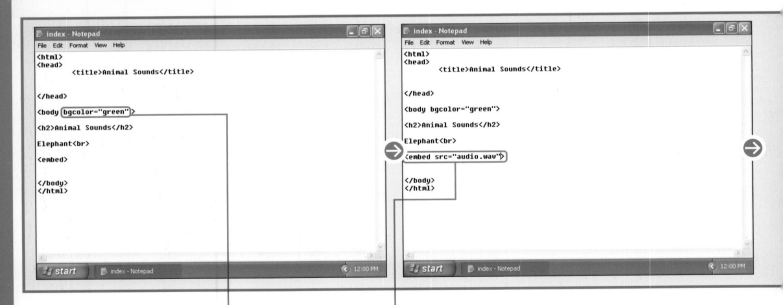

① Open or create an HTML page in a text editor.

② To make the media player easier to see, type the code that changes the Web page background to a darker color.

③ Type **<embed src="?">**, replacing ? with the name of the sound file that you want to play.

Caution! ※

The user viewing your Web page must correctly install and properly configure a media player to listen to your audio file. For this reason, consider using only popular audio formats, such as the .wav format.

Cross-Platform! ※

Different operating systems and Web browsers may use a wide range of media players and media player controls to play audio files. To ensure that all users can access your audio file, you may want to give the user the option of downloading the audio file.

Apply It! ※

Many Web browsers automatically start to play audio files when the Web page loads. To ensure that this happens, include the autostart attribute with the value of true. For example:

```
<embed src="audio.wav" width="300" height="60" autostart="true">
```

DIFFICULTY LEVEL

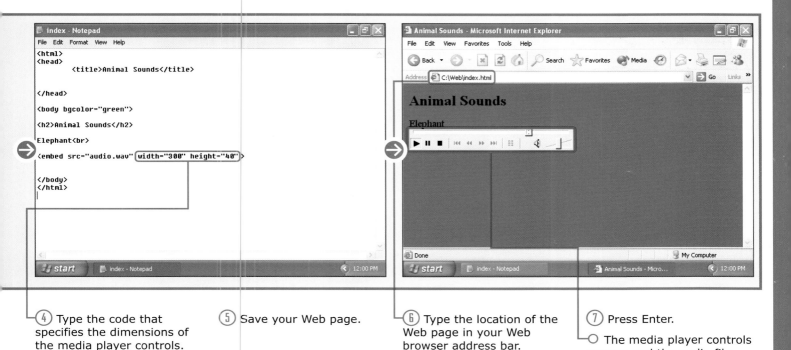

④ Type the code that specifies the dimensions of the media player controls.

⑤ Save your Web page.

⑥ Type the location of the Web page in your Web browser address bar.

⑦ Press Enter.

○ The media player controls appear, and the audio file plays.

EMBED VIDEO
in a Web page

You can embed video clips into your Web page so that users can view them. When you embed video, a media player appears in the Web page, and you specify the size of the media player to accommodate the layout.

You can use the embed tag to display video with the src attribute, which indicates the name of the video file that you want to play. Height and width attributes allow you to specify the video window's size. The size you specify must also include the media player controls, because the height and width is not the true size of the video as it appears on the Web page.

Once the video plays, the user can access the media player controls to play back the video and adjust the volume. Because Web pages do not usually display large video files, try to keep your file size to a few megabytes.

The HTML code that displays video in Web pages often differs depending on the Web browser and the browser's version. For more information about playing video with a specific Web browser, please refer to the Web browser's documentation.

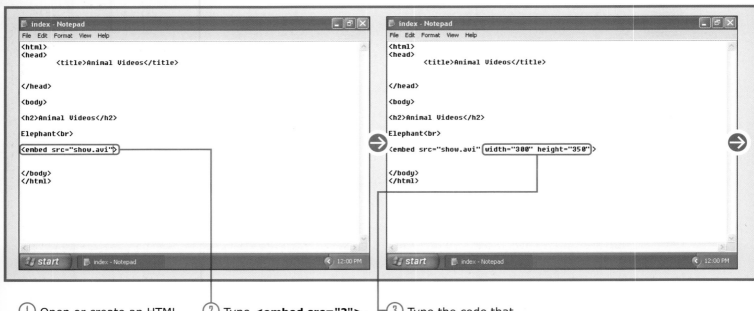

① Open or create an HTML page in a text editor.

② Type **<embed src="?">**, replacing ? with the name of the video you want to play.

③ Type the code that specifies the dimensions of the video player.

Caution!

The video that you embed into a Web page works if the user installs Windows Media Player, and if the video file is in the .avi file format. With other file formats, or computers without Windows Media Player, there is no guarantee that your embedded video will work.

Did You Know?

Although judging the quality of a video is very subjective, there are general guidelines for selecting the dimensions of the video player given the video's quality. Generally, the lower the video quality, the smaller you should make the display window:

Size	Video
Width=160 Height=120	Low quality
Width=240 Height=160	Medium quality
Width=320 Height=240	High quality

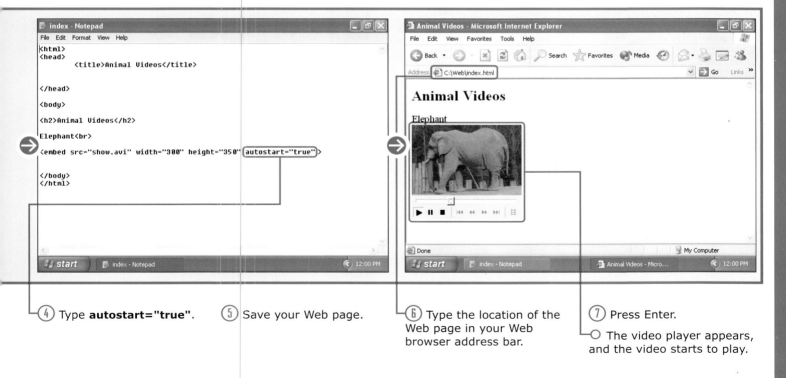

④ Type **autostart="true"**.

⑤ Save your Web page.

⑥ Type the location of the Web page in your Web browser address bar.

⑦ Press Enter.

○ The video player appears, and the video starts to play.

Display
FLASH ANIMATIONS

You can add Flash animations to your Web pages to enhance the appearance of your Web site. Many Web sites use Flash animations to add sound and video such as animated logos and interactive menus.

Flash animations are files that use the .swf file extension. You use the object tag to specify the size of the Flash animation as well as to encapsulate the tag that specifies the name of the Flash animation you want to play.

Within the object start and end tags, the param tag uses the name attribute with the value of movie and

the value attribute to indicate the name of the Flash animation you want to insert into the Web page.

Simply opening the Web page in your Web browser on your own computer may not display the animation. To view the Flash animation, you may need to view your Web page on an actual Web server.

For more detailed information about Flash animations and how to create them, you can refer to the MacroMedia Flash Web site at www.macromedia.com.

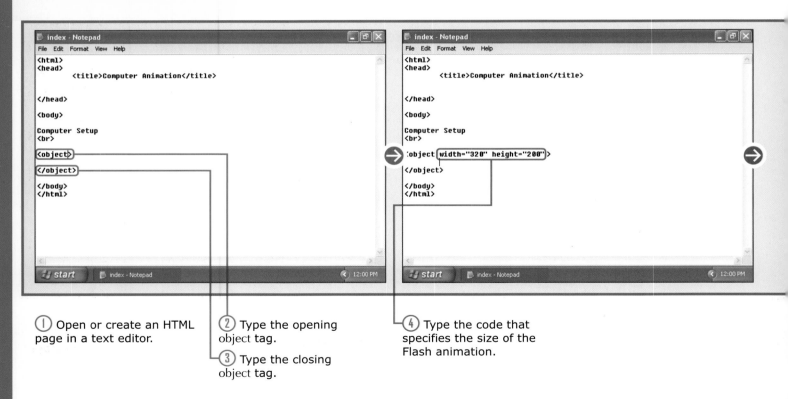

① Open or create an HTML page in a text editor.

② Type the opening object tag.

③ Type the closing object tag.

④ Type the code that specifies the size of the Flash animation.

Apply It!

The width and height
attributes of the object tag allow
you to specify the size of the Flash
animation in pixels or as a percentage of
the Web browser's window width. To specify
the width or height of the Flash animation as a
percentage, simply append the % symbol to the
size value.

Caution!

Many Web browsers cannot play the Flash
animation unless the user installs the
Flash player on his or her computer. For
more information on detecting whether the
Flash player is installed, refer to the main
Flash Web site at www.macromedia.com.

Caution!

Not all Web browsers use the same tag to display
Flash animations. For more detailed information
on displaying Flash animations in different Web
browsers, refer to the Web browser documentation.

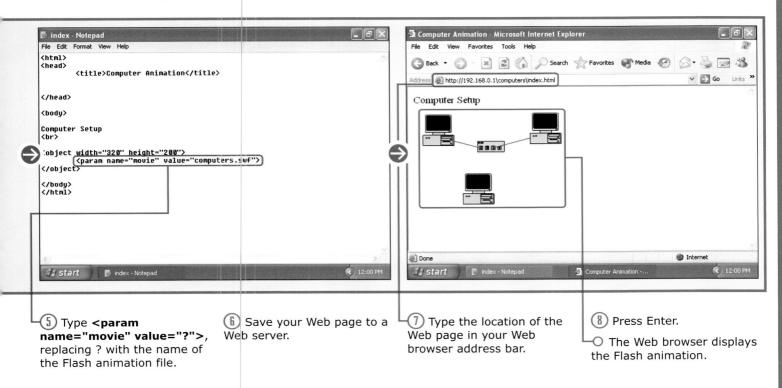

⑤ Type **<param
name="movie" value="?">**,
replacing ? with the name of
the Flash animation file.

⑥ Save your Web page to a
Web server.

⑦ Type the location of the
Web page in your Web
browser address bar.

⑧ Press Enter.

◯ The Web browser displays
the Flash animation.

FRAME Your Web Page

Frames allow you to divide a Web page into multiple sections that each display a separate Web page. Web pages that contain frames can be simple, containing two or three frames, or quite complex, containing many frames of different sizes and shapes.

Frames are extremely useful when you want to keep some information on a Web page fixed and non-changing, while at the same time allowing other content on the page to change. For example, you can use frames to display a banner across the top of all the Web pages on your site that remains the same no matter which Web page a user views.

You create frames by using a simple Web page with a frameset tag, which

encompasses a frame tag. The frameset tag specifies the number of frames to create on the Web page and their size. The Web browser does not actually display the Web page that contains the frameset tag; the frameset tag purely instructs the Web browser how to render the frames. Each frame tag enclosed in a frameset tag contains information about the frame, including the name of the Web page to display in the frame.

You can use any Web page that a Web browser displays as the content of a frame. Web pages that you display in frames are independent of the other Web pages that display in adjoining frames.

TOP 100

<td>
<tbody> <thead> <tr>
<table>

Create a
NAVIGATION FRAME

You can use a navigation frame to make it easier to view a collection of Web pages.

To create a frames-based Web site, you first create a Web page that contains the frameset tag. This tag specifies the number and size of the frames. For a navigation menu you need two frames: a menu frame for the menu items, and a main frame to display the Web pages that the user chooses from the menu items.

For side-by-side frames, you can use the cols attribute of the frameset tag to specify the width of the frames.

For each frame, the frame tag specifies the Web page that appears in the frame as well as the name of the frame.

For the navigation menu to work, each menu item requires a corresponding Web page that appears in the main frame.

The Web page that contains the menu items has simple links that you create with the a tag. The a tag contains the target attribute that identifies the frame, which displays the Web page, namely the main frame.

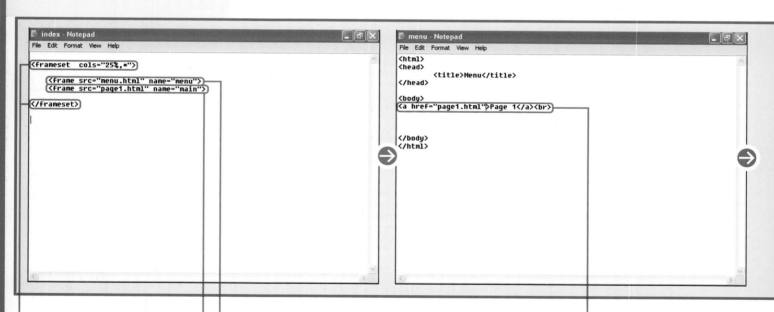

① Type the opening and closing frameset tags to create a Web page with two frames.

② Type the code that names the menu frame and specifies which Web page appears in that frame.

③ Type the code that names the main frame and specifies which Web page appears in that frame.

④ Save the Web page.

⑤ Open or create the Web page that you want to appear in the menu frame.

⑥ Type the code that creates a link to another Web page.

Did You Know? ※

You can create frames that divide the Web page horizontally instead of vertically by using the rows attribute instead of the cols attribute of the frameset tag. For example:

```
<frameset rows="25%,*">
```

DIFFICULTY LEVEL

Apply It! ※

Although many browsers can use frames, some older browsers cannot. You can create a message that appears when an older browser that cannot work with frames accesses your Web page. Simply include a noframes tag within the opening and closing frameset tag. Any text between the opening and closing noframes tag displays in the browser window. For example:

```
<noframes>Frames not enabled</noframes>
```

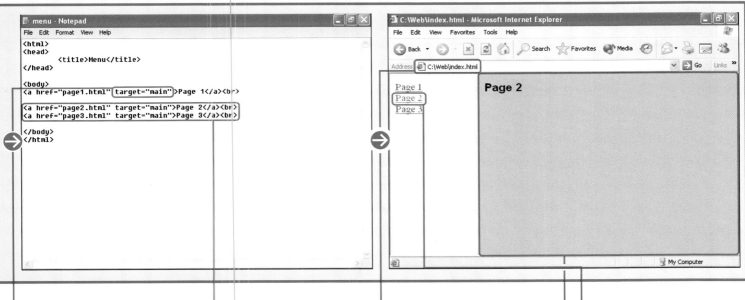

⑦ Type **target="?"**, replacing ? with the name of the main frame that you specify in step **3**.

⑧ Repeat steps **6** and **7** for each additional Web page in the menu.

⑨ Save your menu page.

⑩ Type the location of the Web page in your Web browser address bar.

⑪ Press Enter.

⑫ Click an item in the menu.

○ The corresponding Web page appears in the main frame.

Secure a frame border to
CONTROL WEB PAGE LAYOUT

You can prevent users from moving a frame border. Normally, users can easily resize a frame by clicking and dragging the borders of the frame to a new location. Resizing a frame can sometimes totally obscure the content of the frame. If your Web page contains frames that have images, menus or other items of a fixed size, you should secure the frame border to ensure that the frame is always large enough to display the entire contents of the frame.

In this way, securing all the frames on a Web page allows you to control the layout of frame-enabled Web pages.

You can secure a frame border using the noresize attribute of the frame tag. Unlike many other tag attributes, the noresize attribute has no values.

When you secure a frame border, you also secure any common borders with other frames, regardless of whether the noresize attribute is set in the other frames.

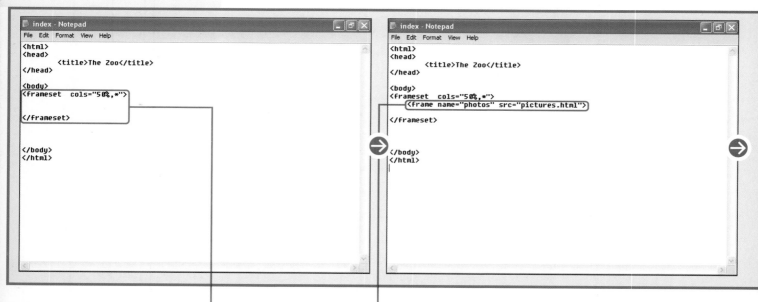

① Create or open the main Web page that you want to contain the frame information.

② Type the code that contains the opening and closing frameset tags.

③ Type the code to create a frame.

#44

Did You Know? ※

When designing Web pages that use secure borders, you must test the appearance of the Web pages at different resolutions. The sizes that you specify for the frame dimensions may look acceptable at high resolution but may not appear as you intended at low resolutions. To fully see how frames appear for a wide range of users, test your Web page using multiple Web browsers.

Apply It! ※

You can secure the borders of just one frame in a Web page while allowing the user to move the borders of other frames. For example, if you place a menu in a frame across the top of a Web page, you can secure that frame while allowing the user to horizontally resize other frames under the menu frame.

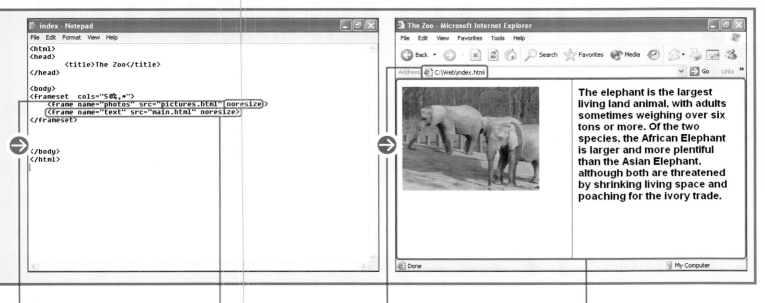

④ Type **noresize** in the frame tag.

⑤ Repeat steps **3** and **4** for each frame that you want to create.

⑥ Save your Web page.

⑦ Type the location of the Web page in your Web browser address bar.

⑧ Press Enter.

○ In the Web page that appears, you cannot move the frame border.

Display one Web page within another with
INLINE FRAMES

You can insert a frame into the content of a Web page to display one Web page within another Web page. When you do this, you create an *inline frame*.

You create inline frames using the iframe tag. The iframe tag uses the src attribute to specify the name of the Web page you want to display in the inline frame. You should make the Web pages that appear in an inline frame small enough to display adequately within the smaller inline frame. If the

content of the inline frame does not fit, a scrollbar at the side of the inline frame allows the user to move up and down through the Web page that displays in the inline frame.

Unlike other frames, users cannot resize inline frames. Although some older Web browsers may not support the use of inline frames, a user can view them in Internet Explorer, the most popular Web browser.

① Create or open a Web page that you want to contain an inline frame.

② Type the code that adds content to your Web page.

③ Type the opening and closing iframe tags.

Did You Know? ※

You can specify the size of an inline frame. Using the width and height attributes within the opening iframe tag, specify the frame dimensions in pixels or as a percentage of the Web browser window by appending the % symbol to the width and height values.

Did You Know? ※

You can disable the scroll bar of an inline frame by adding the attribute and value scrolling="no" to the opening iframe tag.

Customize It! ※

Some Web browsers may not fully support the iframe tag. You can place text, such as a warning, between the opening and closing iframe tags, that appears in browsers that do not support inline frames. For example:

```
<iframe src="text.html">
    This page uses inline frames
</iframe>
```

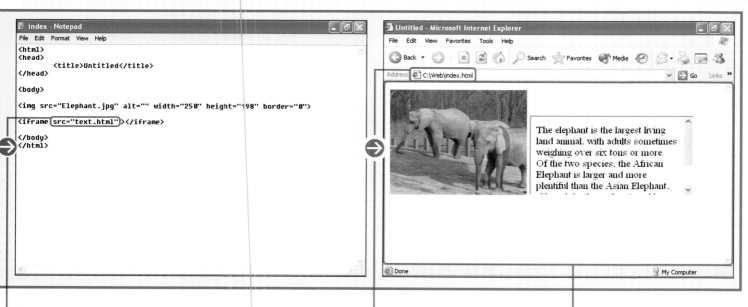

④ Type **src="?"** in the opening iframe tag, replacing ? with the name of the Web page that you want to appear in the inline frame.

⑤ Save your Web page.

⑥ Type the location of the Web page in your Web browser address bar.

⑦ Press Enter.

○ The Web page appears, containing the inline frame.

CREATE A MESSAGE
for non-frame browsers and search engines

When you create Web pages that use frames, you can still display information in Web browsers that do not support frames. Older Web browsers often do not display frame-enabled Web pages, and some users may use Web browsers with frame support turned off.

When search engines scan Web pages, they look for information about the Web pages in order to catalog them. However, Web pages that contain frame instructions do not contain any content, making it

difficult for the search engine to catalog the page correctly. If you make text available to non-frame-enabled Web browsers, search engines can use this text to catalog your Web page more accurately.

You can place content that you want to appear in non-frame-enabled Web browsers in the noframes tag within the frameset tags that create the frames of the Web page. You can make the contents of the noframes tag any valid HTML code, including text, images, and links.

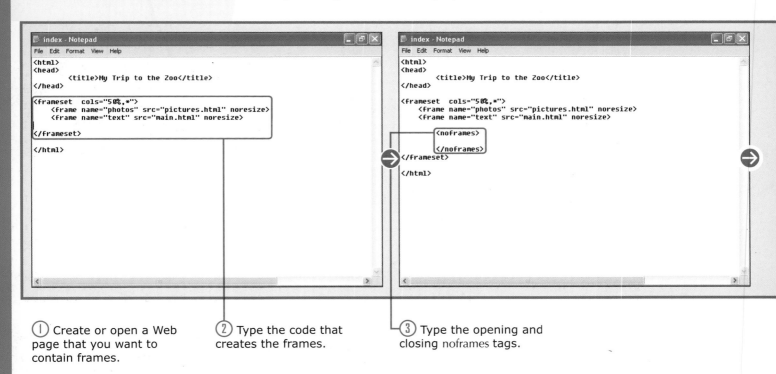

① Create or open a Web page that you want to contain frames.

② Type the code that creates the frames.

③ Type the opening and closing noframes tags.

Did You Know? ※

When you view frames in a frame-enabled Web browser, the browser ignores any information you include in the noframes tag. To view the information in the noframes tag, use the Web browser to display the source code of the Web page.

Apply It! ※

Some Web pages that use a complex frame configuration may use more than one frameset tag to set up the frames of the Web page. You should place the noframes tag in the outermost, or first, occurrence of the frameset tag.

'd You Know? ※

You do not need to use the noframes tag, however, any Web browser that does not display frames will simply display a blank page whenever it views a Web page with frames.

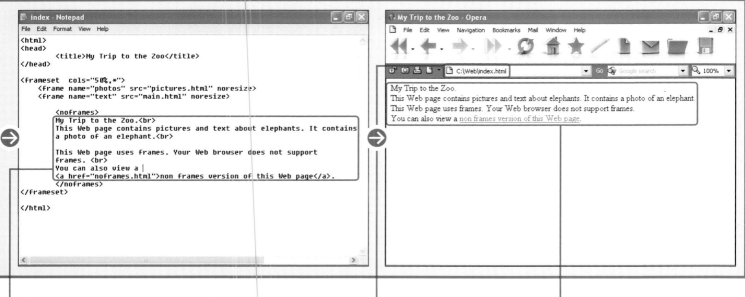

④ Type the code that you want to appear when a browser does not support frames.

⑤ Save your Web page.

⑥ Type the location of the Web page in your Web browser address bar.

○ This example uses the Opera Web browser with frames support disabled.

⑦ Press Enter.

○ Text appears for browsers that do not support frames.

TURNING OFF SCROLL BARS

When the content of a frame is larger than the frame area, a scroll bar automatically appears at the right side or the bottom of the frame. This enables the user to easily scroll up or down or from side to side through the frame content. You can eliminate scroll bars from a frame to ensure that the content of the frame appears in the maximum possible area of the frame.

You can turn off the scroll bar by adding the scrolling attribute to the frame tag for the frame you do not want to scroll. To turn off scrolling, you can set the value of the scrolling attribute to No.

When turning off scroll bars, you cannot choose between turning off the scroll bar at the bottom or the right of the frame, you can only choose whether you want to show scroll bars.

Keep in mind that when you turn off the scroll bar, and the information in the frame does not display entirely, the user cannot resize the frame to view the frame's entire contents.

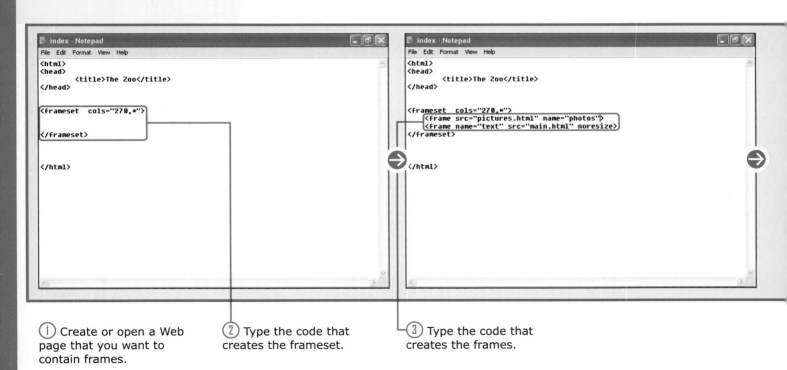

① Create or open a Web page that you want to contain frames.

② Type the code that creates the frameset.

③ Type the code that creates the frames.

Did You Know? ※

If you create a Web page that uses frames and you want to display scroll bars, even if the content of the frame does not require it, you can easily force the frame to display a scroll bar by specifying the value of Yes for the scrolling attribute of the frame tag.

Did You Know? ※

If you turn off scroll bars to better control the area and layout of the contents of a frame, the layout may change when you view the Web page at different resolutions or with different Web browsers. Always ensure that you test the layout of your Web page at different resolutions and, if possible, with different Web browsers.

DIFFICULTY LEVEL

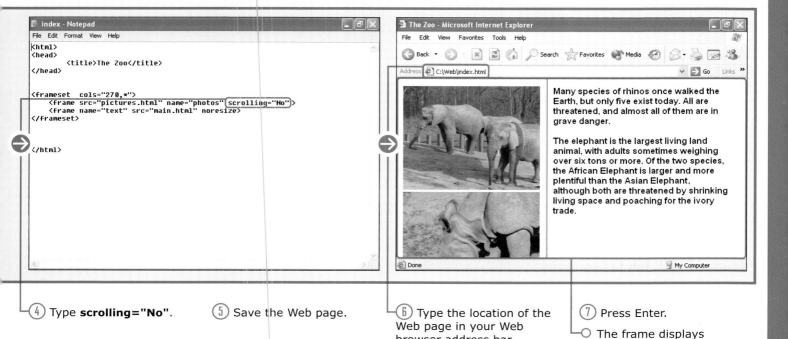

④ Type **scrolling="No"**.

⑤ Save the Web page.

⑥ Type the location of the Web page in your Web browser address bar.

⑦ Press Enter.

○ The frame displays without scrollbars.

Force the
USE OF FRAMES

You can force a Web page to appear within a frame of another Web page. When you design a Web page to appear within a frame, users can directly access that page by entering the Web page address in the address bar of a Web browser.

You can force a Web page to appear within a frame by using a simple JavaScript script. The script accesses the name of the Web page currently appearing in the Web browser. If the Web page that appears is not the Web page that contains the frame

information, then the Web browser loads the Web page that creates and displays the frames. The script makes a decision using an if statement that tests a condition, and then processes a line of code if the condition is true.

Because your browser processes the code before it displays the Web page, the JavaScript script that forces the use of frames must appear within the head section of the HTML code within a script tag.

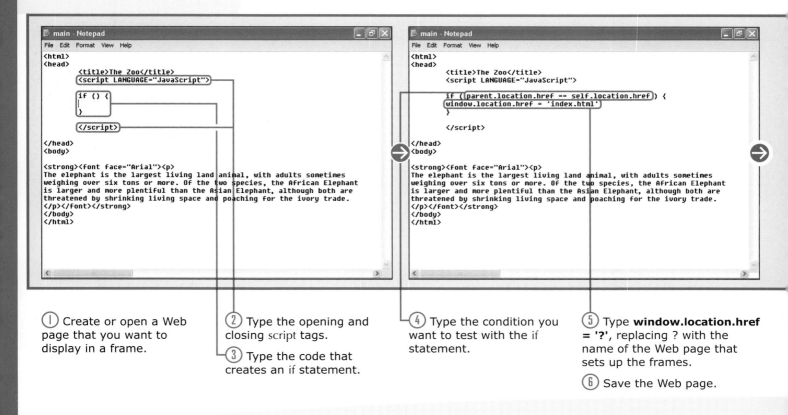

① Create or open a Web page that you want to display in a frame.

② Type the opening and closing script tags.

③ Type the code that creates an if statement.

④ Type the condition you want to test with the if statement.

⑤ Type **window.location.href = '?'**, replacing ? with the name of the Web page that sets up the frames.

⑥ Save the Web page.

Did You Know? ※

Most programming languages, including JavaScript, use two equal to signs (==) instead of one when comparing two values within an if statement. This prevents confusion when assigning values to variables where you use a single equal to sign, as in age=25.

Apply It! ※

JavaScript uses *variables* to store information about the Web pages the Web browser is currently displaying:

Common JavaScript Variables	
Variable	*Description*
parent.location.href	The initial Web page that displays.
self.location.href	The Web page that contains the script.
window.location.href	The Web page that the browser loads.

48

DIFFICULTY LEVEL

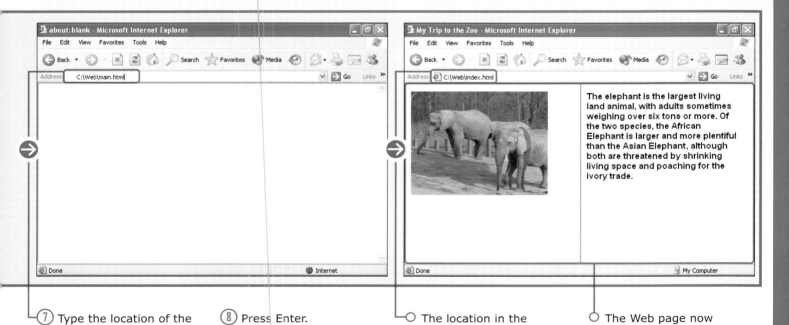

⑦ Type the location of the Web page in your Web browser address bar.

⑧ Press Enter.

○ The location in the browser changes to the Web page you specified in step **5**.

○ The Web page now appears in a frame.

Break out of a frame to
FULLY DISPLAY A WEB PAGE

When you restore a Web page to the full display of the Web browser, you refer to this as *breaking a Web page out of a frame*. You can force a Web page to break out of a frame and to display in the full area of the Web browser.

Some Web sites that create links to your Web pages may link to your Web page within a frame, allowing a user to view and navigate your Web site while still displaying the Web page from the original site in another frame. For example, this technique can

display advertising to a user, which you do not control, while the user is accessing the Web, including your site.

A JavaScript script determines whether the Web page that appears is the topmost page that displays. If the script detects another topmost page, it instructs the Web browser to reload the current Web page as the topmost page. You must place the JavaScript script within the head section of the HTML code of the Web page.

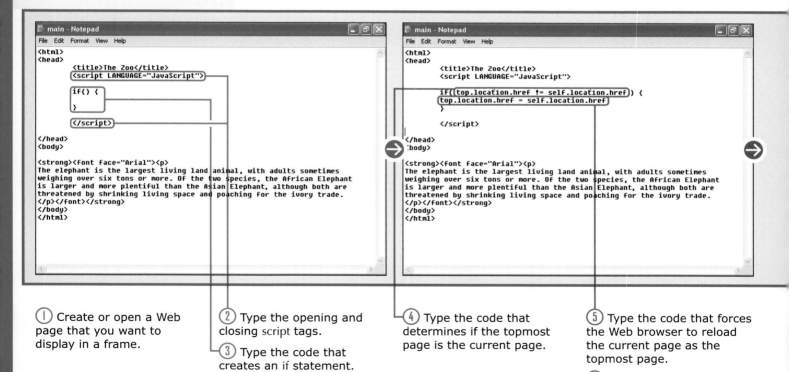

① Create or open a Web page that you want to display in a frame.

② Type the opening and closing script tags.

③ Type the code that creates an if statement.

④ Type the code that determines if the topmost page is the current page.

⑤ Type the code that forces the Web browser to reload the current page as the topmost page.

⑥ Save the Web page.

Did You Know? ☀

JavaScript determines which Web page appears as the topmost page by using an if statement to analyze whether two items are not equal. Most programming languages, including JavaScript, use the != characters to indicate inequality.

Customize It! ☀

If you do not want to automatically break a Web page out of a frame, you can let your user choose to break out the Web page by using a link to load the current Web page into the topmost frame. Change the name of the link to the Web page to the name of the Web page that contains the link. For example:

```
<a href="main.html" target="_top">Break out</a>
```

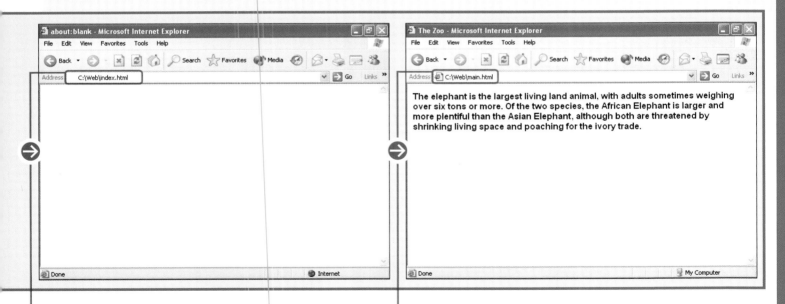

⑦ Type the location of the Web page that contains a frame, which displays the Web page you saved in step **6**.

⑧ Press Enter.

○ The location in the Web browser changes to the Web page containing the JavaScript script.

○ The Web page now appears in the Web browser window.

CHAPTER 6

Get Interactive with Forms

You can use forms to allow users to interact with your Web site. A form typically consists of *fields* where users type data. Once the users type the information, they then click a submit button that sends the data to the Web server.

A program or a script on the Web server must process the data that a user enters in a form. You can create your own programs or scripts to process form data if you know how to program. Many Web-hosting servers provide easily accessible programs that process form data. If you do not have a method of processing form data, you cannot use forms on your Web site.

You can design and create forms on your own computer without the use of a forms data processing program using the HTML form tag. The form tag specifies the name of the program or script on the Web server that processes the form data. In addition to fields where users type data, you can also use radio buttons and checkboxes to allow users to select options. Keep in mind that the Web browser you use affects the appearance of the forms and form buttons, which may look slightly different from browser to browser.

Form data passes to the Web server with either the get or post method, which you specify as the value of the forms method attribute. You usually pass small amounts of information using the get method.

TOP 100

<td>
<tbody> <thead> <tr>
<table>

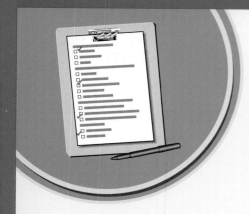

Permit users to
CLEAR A FORM'S CONTENT

You can allow users to erase information they entered in a form. By doing so, users can revise or correct any errors in the form data before they submit the information to the Web server. Clear buttons are especially useful on forms that contain numerous text areas. When a user selects the clear button, all information erases regardless of whether the user has partially or fully completed the form.

You can use the input tag with the type attribute set to rest to create a button that the user clicks to clear the form. A value attribute contains the text that you

want to appear on the button. As with the tag that creates the submit button, the input tag does not require a closing tag.

You can use one clear button for each form, and if you have multiple forms on one Web page, the clear button only works on the form data to which the clear button belongs.

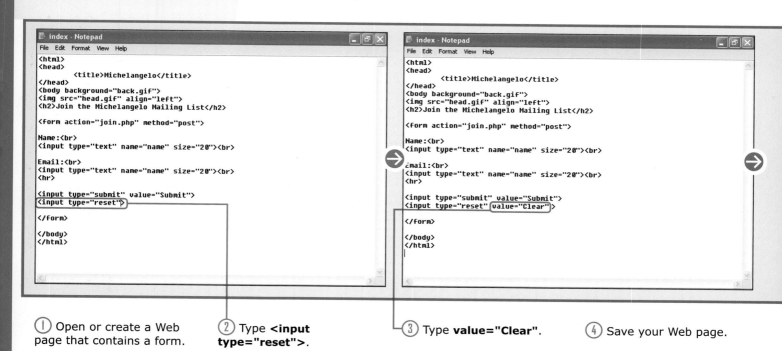

① Open or create a Web page that contains a form.

② Type **<input type="reset">**.

③ Type **value="Clear"**.

④ Save your Web page.

Caution! ※

There is no way for users to recover data once they clear it from a form. If you are creating a large form with many fields where users enter data, you may want to break the form down into smaller sections and place them on different Web pages.

Caution! ※

Always make sure that the clear data button and the submit data button are easily distinguishable from each other. Otherwise, users may inadvertently click the clear button instead of the submit button. You may even want to ensure that there is adequate distance between both buttons on the Web page to prevent the user from accidentally clicking the clear button.

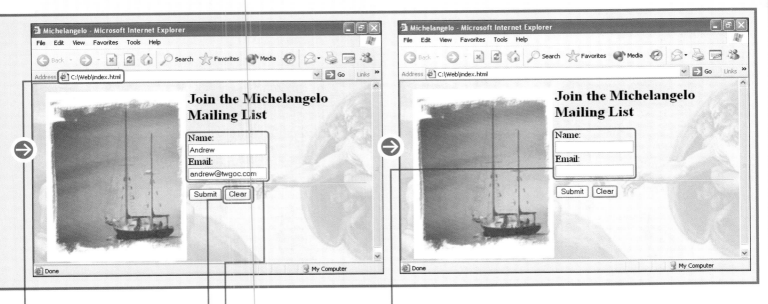

⑤ Type the location of the Web page in your Web browser address bar.

⑥ Press Enter.

⑦ Type information into the form fields.

⑧ Click Clear.

○ The Web browser clears the information in the form.

Create a
DROP-DOWN LIST

You can create a drop-down list to allow users of your Web page to make a selection from a number of items. A drop-down list consists of two tags: the select tag establishes the drop-down list, while the option tag identifies the items in the list.

The size attribute of the select tag specifies the height of the drop-down list. For a standard drop-down list, the normal height is one line.

Each option tag encloses the text that you want to appear in the drop-down menu. The value attribute

stores the value that passes to the Web server when a user selects the option. The script that processes the information in the form must then properly interpret what the values represent.

When the drop-down list appears on the Web page, the first item displays and is automatically selected. To select a new item, the user clicks a down-arrow to reveal the other items in the list. You can place as many items in the drop-down list as you want.

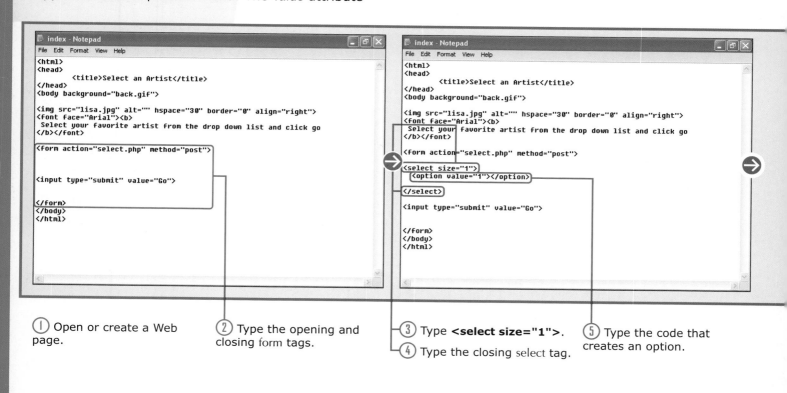

① Open or create a Web page.

② Type the opening and closing form tags.

③ Type **<select size="1">**.

④ Type the closing select tag.

⑤ Type the code that creates an option.

51

Apply It!

If you have one particular item in the drop-down list that users select more than others, you can use the selected attribute in the option tag to have the item selected by default when the drop-down list appears on the Web page:

```
<option value="2" selected>Pablo Picasso</option>
```

Apply It!

If you want users to select multiple items from the drop-down list, you can use the multiple attribute in the select tag. The drop-down list now displays as a list rather than a drop-down list, and users can select multiple items by holding down the Ctrl key while clicking items in the list. For example:

```
<select name="" size="3" multiple>
```

index - Notepad

File   Edit   Format   View   Help

```
<html>
<head>
        <title>Select an Artist</title>
</head>
<body background="back.gif">

<img src="lisa.jpg" alt="" hspace="30" border="0" align="right">
<font face="Arial"><b>
  Select your favorite artist from the drop down list and click go
</b></font>

<form action="select.php" method="post">

<select size="1">
   <option value="1">Michelangelo</option>
   <option value="2">Pablo Picasso</option>
   <option value="3">Vincent Van Gogh</option>
   <option value="4">Leonardo Da Vinci</option>
</select>

<input type="submit" value="Go">

</form>
</body>
</html>
```

Select an Artist - Microsoft Internet Explorer

File   Edit   View   Favorites   Tools   Help

Back   Search   Favorites   Media

Address   C:\Web\index.html   Go   Links

Select your favorite artist from the drop down list and click go

Michelangelo   Go

Michelangelo
Pablo Picasso
Vincent Van Gogh
Leonardo Da Vinci

Done   My Computer

⑥ Type the text you want to appear in the option.

⑦ Repeat steps **5** and **6** for each item in the drop-down list.

⑧ Save your Web page.

⑨ Type the location of the Web page in your Web browser address bar.

⑩ Press Enter.

⑪ Click the down-arrow.

○ A list of choices appears.

IMAGE AS A BUTTON

Each form requires a submit button that the user can click in order to send the information in the form to the Web server. When you create a submit button using HTML code, it appears as a rectangular gray button with black text. You can enhance the look of your Web page by changing the submit button to an image. You can create the image that you want to use as a button in an image-editing program.

To use an image as a button, you can still use the input tag, but you must set the type value to image. You can then use the src attribute to specify the name of the image file you want to use as a button.

You must place the input tag within the start and end form tags of the form on which you want to use the button. If you prefer, you can use attributes normally available to image tags such as height, width, and border.

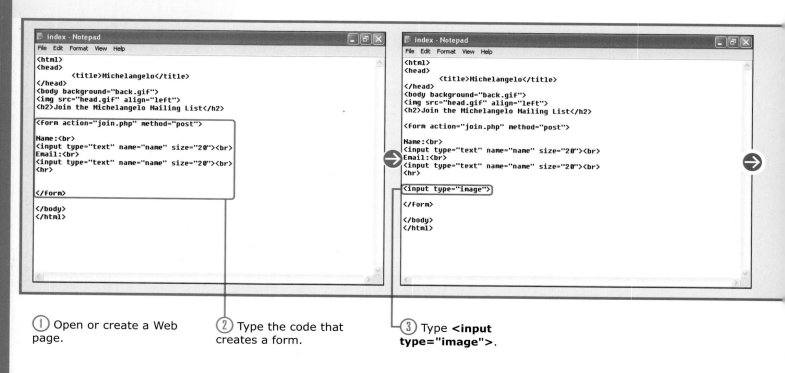

① Open or create a Web page.

② Type the code that creates a form.

③ Type **<input type="image">**.

52

Caution! ※

When you use images as buttons, you must ensure that any image you create is clearly recognizable as a button. If the image does not look like a button, a user may not understand the function of the image.

Apply It! ※

When you create an image for use as a button, you can save the file in any file format that a Web browser can display. Most users save buttons as GIF images because of their small file size.

Did You Know? ※

You can still use an input tag to create a Clear button, even if the submit button is an image. For more on Clear buttons, see task #50.

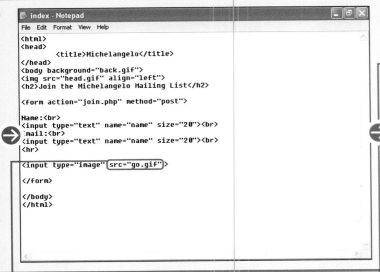

④ Type **src="?"**, replacing ? with the name of the image.

⑤ Save your Web page.

⑥ Type the location of the Web page in your Web browser address bar.

⑦ Press Enter.

○ The image button appears.

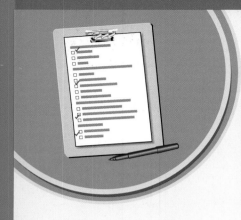

PLACE DEFAULT TEXT
in a form

You can place information in a form to instruct the user on the form's function and use. The appearance of the default text that you place in the form depends on the type of field that the form has. Some fields consist of one line of text, while other fields require that users type in many lines of text.

When you create a form field with the input tag, you can add a value attribute to the input tag. The value of the value attribute is the default text that you

want to appear in the field when the form appears in a Web browser.

A text area field allows you to create an area where a user can enter larger amounts of text. You must use the textarea tag to generate the field, and you must use an opening and closing tag. You can then place the default text that you want to appear in the text area between the opening and closing textarea tags.

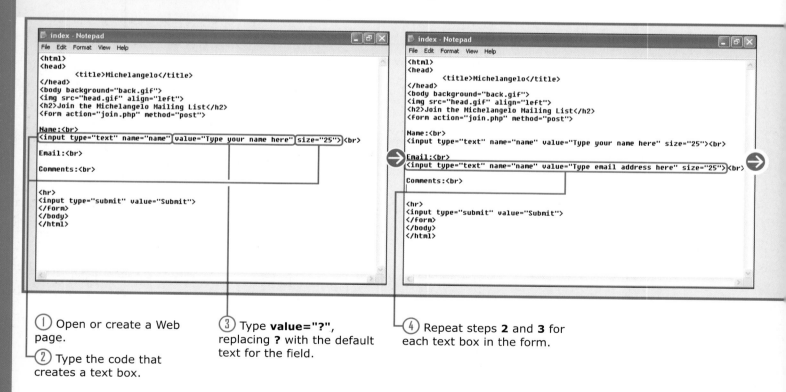

① Open or create a Web page.

② Type the code that creates a text box.

③ Type **value="?"**, replacing **?** with the default text for the field.

④ Repeat steps **2** and **3** for each text box in the form.

Did You Know? ※

Users can either replace the default text in a text field, or they can alter it and append new text to it. Any information in the form fields passes to the Web server when the users press the submit button, regardless of whether they add text or leave the default text.

Apply It! ※

You can use other elements to select default values. For example, when creating checkboxes, if you add the checked attribute to the input tag, the checkbox will contain a check mark when it appears on the form. The user can then leave it checked or uncheck it. For example:

```
<input type="checkbox" value ="yes" name="mailer" checked>
```

DIFFICULTY LEVEL

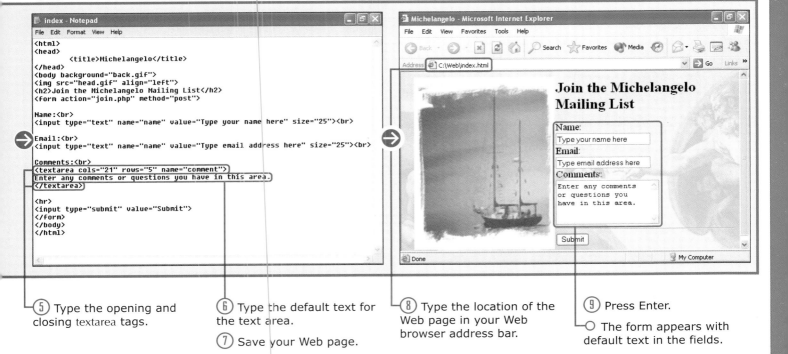

⑤ Type the opening and closing textarea tags.

⑥ Type the default text for the text area.

⑦ Save your Web page.

⑧ Type the location of the Web page in your Web browser address bar.

⑨ Press Enter.

○ The form appears with default text in the fields.

Create
SHORTCUT KEYS
to select checkboxes

You can create keyboard shortcuts to allow users to quickly select items on your Web page. Shortcut keys are very useful if your form contains a lot of checkboxes, as they allow users quick access to the options they want to select.

To use a shortcut key, the user must press and hold down the Alt key and then press another key on the keyboard. When using shortcut keys with forms, users must always use the Alt key.

You can create a shortcut key by adding the accesskey attribute to the input tag that you use to

create the checkbox. The value of the accesskey attribute is a single character, representing the key that you use in combination with the Alt key to create the shortcut. You can specify either a number or a letter as the accesskey value.

You must indicate to users what shortcut keys they can use with the form. In most cases, you simply append the shortcut description to the end of the text that describes the checkbox.

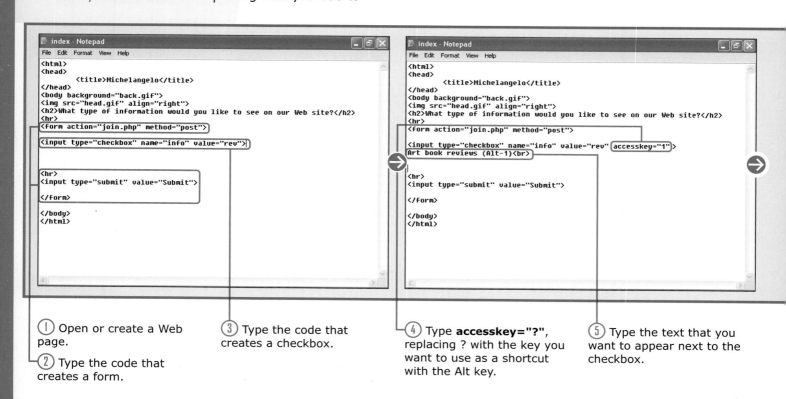

① Open or create a Web page.

② Type the code that creates a form.

③ Type the code that creates a checkbox.

④ Type **accesskey="?"**, replacing ? with the key you want to use as a shortcut with the Alt key.

⑤ Type the text that you want to appear next to the checkbox.

120

54

DIFFICULTY LEVEL

Caution! ☀
Although the current version of Internet Explorer does support the accesskey attribute, many older browsers do not.

Caution! ☀
You can use numbers or letters when specifying the shortcut key in conjunction with the Alt key. When specifying letters, you must be careful not to choose a key combination that conflicts with another function of the Web browser. For example, many Internet Explorer versions use the Alt-P key combination to set printing options and to print the currently displayed Web page; therefore you can never use this as a shortcut key for your forms. Few Web browsers use the Alt key in combination with numbers, so, if possible, you should use numbers when creating shortcuts.

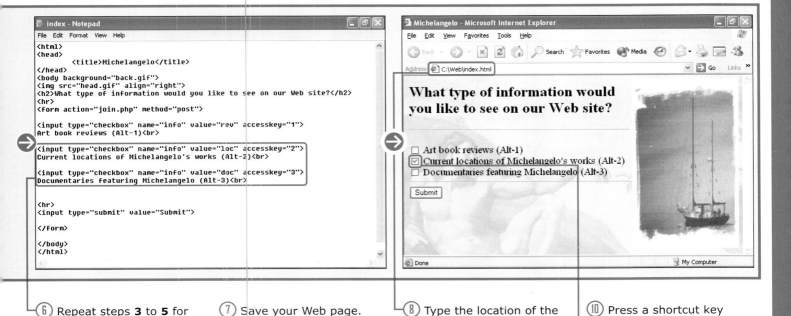

⑥ Repeat steps **3** to **5** for each checkbox you want to create.

⑦ Save your Web page.

⑧ Type the location of the Web page in your Web browser address bar.

⑨ Press Enter.

⑩ Press a shortcut key combination.

○ A check mark appears in the checkbox you select.

RESTRICT TEXT SIZE
in a form

You can limit the amount of information a user can enter into a form to avoid the entry of unnecessary information. Restricting the number of characters in an input tag for a form prevents users from inadvertently entering large amounts of data. This is important because large amounts of data in a form may adversely affect the program that processes the form data.

The maxlength attribute of the input tag restricts the number of characters that a user can type in a field. If the user attempts to enter more characters than

you allow, these characters simply do not appear when a user types them.

While you can specify the size of an input field on a form, this only affects the size of the field as it appears on the Web page. It does not limit the number of characters a user can type in the field. When the number of characters that a user types is larger than the field can display, the text field simply scrolls to allow the user to continue entering data.

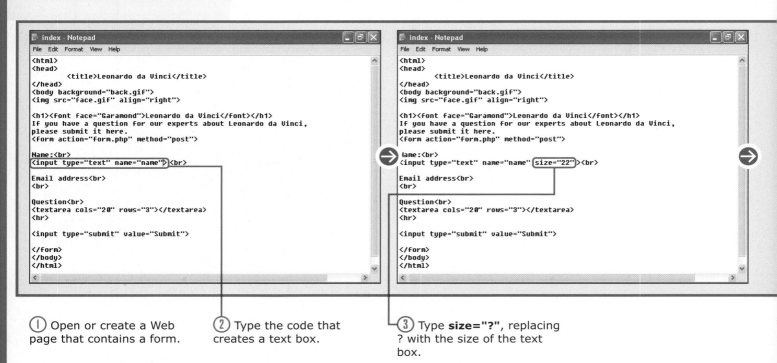

① Open or create a Web page that contains a form.

② Type the code that creates a text box.

③ Type **size="?"**, replacing ? with the size of the text box.

DIFFICULTY LEVEL

Apply It! ※

You should coordinate
the amount of data that a
user can enter into a form with
the program or script that eventually
processes the data from the form. For
example, if a script processes e-mail
addresses submitted on a form, and only allows
30 characters for the e-mail address, the form
should allow no more than 30 characters in the field
where the users type e-mail addresses.

Apply It! ※

You can use the size attribute to make
the size of a field on a Web page larger
than the length of the allowed text, which
you specify with the maxlength attribute. This
allows users to see all the text that they type.

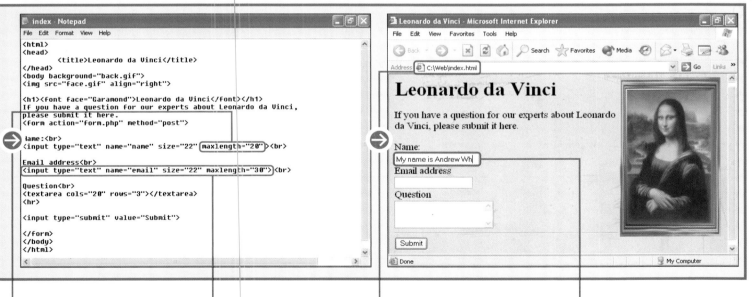

④ Type **maxlength="?"**,
replacing ? with the
maximum number of
characters you want
to allow.

⑤ Repeat steps **2** to **4** for
each text box you want to
create.

⑥ Save your Web page.

⑦ Type the location of the
Web page in your Web
browser address bar.

⑧ Press Enter.

⑨ Type your text in the
text box.

○ When you reach the
maximum text size, any
additional text you type
does not appear.

Protect information by
HIDING TYPED DATA

You can prevent others from viewing information that users enter on a Web page form by masking the characters as the user types them. *Masking* is the process of replacing each typed character with another symbol.

You can use the input tag to create a password field that hides text as users type it. To do this, you must set the type attribute of the input tag to the value password.

When creating a password field, you should keep the required amount of text to a minimum to prevent

users from making errors while typing. Password fields are typically no larger than ten characters.

The actual character that appears when the user types a character in a password field depends on the operating system and the Web browser. Some Web browsers replace each character that the user types with an asterisk, while other Web browsers may use a small circle.

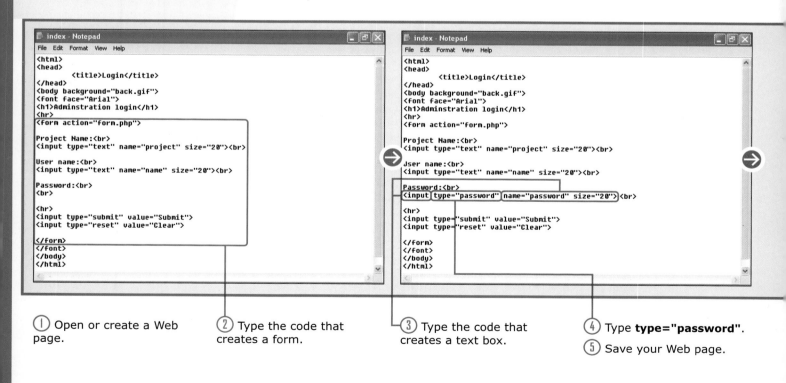

```
index - Notepad
File  Edit  Format  View  Help
<html>
<head>
        <title>Login</title>
</head>
<body background="back.gif">
<font face="Arial">
<h1>Adminstration login</h1>
<hr>
<form action="form.php">

Project Name:<br>
<input type="text" name="project" size="20"><br>

User name:<br>
<input type="text" name="name" size="20"><br>

Password:<br>
<br>

<hr>
<input type="submit" value="Submit">
<input type="reset" value="Clear">

</form>
</font>
</body>
</html>
```

```
index - Notepad
File  Edit  Format  View  Help
<html>
<head>
        <title>Login</title>
</head>
<body background="back.gif">
<font face="Arial">
<h1>Adminstration login</h1>
<hr>
<form action="form.php">

Project Name:<br>
<input type="text" name="project" size="20"><br>

Jser name:<br>
<input type="text" name="name" size="20"><br>

Password:<br>
<input type="password" name="password" size="20"><br>

<hr>
<input type="submit" value="Submit">
<input type="reset" value="Clear">

</form>
</font>
</body>
</html>
```

① Open or create a Web page.

② Type the code that creates a form.

③ Type the code that creates a text box.

④ Type **type="password"**.

⑤ Save your Web page.

Caution! ☀

While a password field prevents the casual passerby from viewing information that you type, it is not a secure way to handle sensitive data. There are still many ways in which others can intercept and view the data that you enter in a password field.

Apply It! ☀

Although the input type for a field is set to password, you can still use the size and maxlength attributes to restrict the display size of the field and the amount of data users can type. When restricting the length of text that users can type into a password field, you should ensure that the users know of these restrictions. To set the size and maxlength values, simply include the attributes in the password tag:

```
<input type="password" name="pass" size="2" maxlength="10">
```

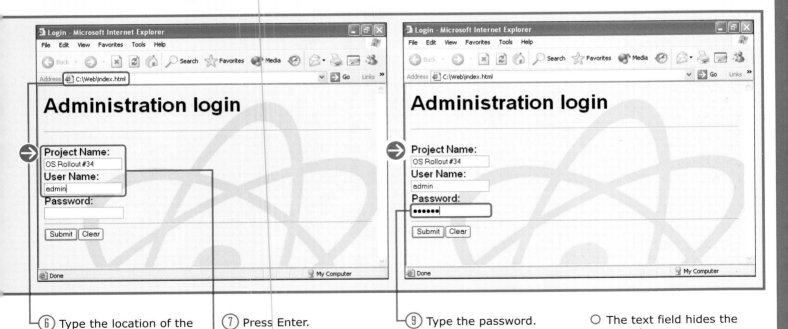

⑥ Type the location of the Web page in your Web browser address bar.

⑦ Press Enter.

⑧ Type the information that the form requires.

⑨ Type the password.

○ The text field hides the password.

Change how
WORDS WRAP
in the text area

When a user types information into a text area field on your Web page, you can change the way that this information appears in the field. Normally, when the line of text reaches the right side of the text area, the text *wraps*, or moves to the next line. However, you can change the text area setting so that the text wraps to a new line whenever the user wants it to instead of when the text reaches the right margin of the text area.

To turn off the wrap in a text area, you can add the wrap attribute to the textarea tag and set the value to

off. Now, when a user types text in a text area, the text scrolls until the user presses Enter, at which point it starts a new line.

You can identify a text area field that has wrapping turned off by the scroll bar at the bottom of the text area. All text area fields have a scroll bar on the right side of the field, regardless of the wrap setting.

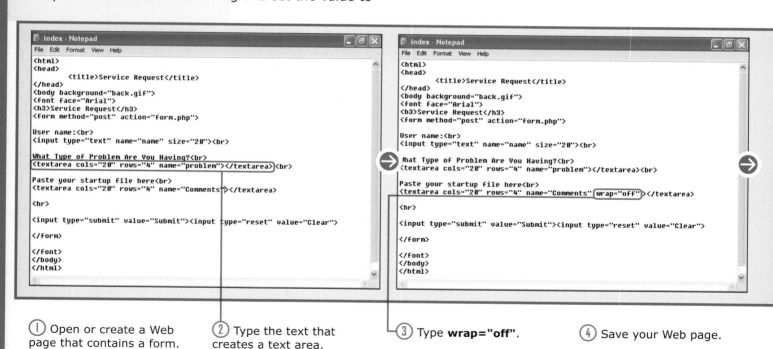

① Open or create a Web page that contains a form.

② Type the text that creates a text area.

③ Type **wrap="off"**.

④ Save your Web page.

#57

Apply It! ※

By default, all text areas wrap text without you having to specify the wrap attribute. If a textarea tag has a wrap attribute, you can turn off the wrapping by changing the value of the wrap attribute to soft.

Apply It! ※

Newline, an invisible character, appears at the end of every line of text. When you set the wrap attribute to soft, or when you have no wrap attribute, the text field inserts newlines when the user presses Enter and starts a new text line. You use the hard value for the wrap attribute to force the Web browser to insert a newline whenever the text wraps in the text area. This makes the text appear the same after processing as it does on the Web page.

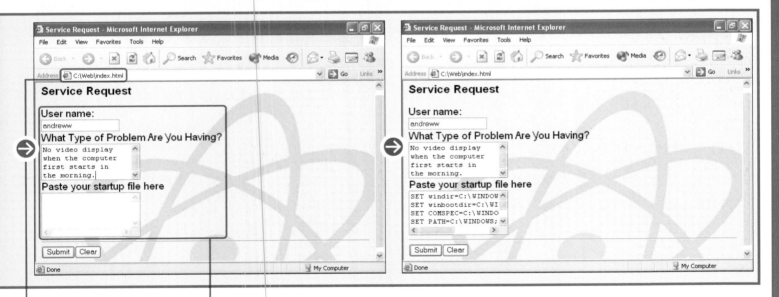

⑤ Type the location of the Web page in your Web browser address bar.

⑥ Press Enter.

⑦ Type text into the form fields.

○ The text scrolls to fill the text area.

Make form text
UNCHANGEABLE

You can place data into form fields and prevent users from changing that data. You can do this to ensure that a user submits specific data, or because you have not yet implemented the field in your Web page. You can make data unchangeable in text boxes or text areas.

There are two ways to make form data unchangeable. If you make text read-only, the user cannot change any default text that appears in the form. When the user submits the form, the Web browser submits any data marked as read-only to

the program or script processing the form data. You make data in a form field unchangeable by adding the readonly attribute to the input or textarea tag.

The second way to make form data unchangeable is to disable the text so that it appears dim in the form. When the user clicks the submit button, the Web browser does not submit any disabled text to the program or script that processes the form data. You can disable data in a form field by adding the disabled attribute to the input or textarea tag.

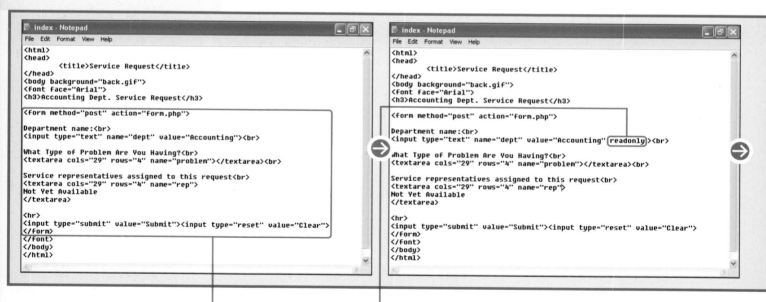

① Open or create a Web page.

② Create a form with a text box and a text area.

③ Type **readonly** in the tag for the text box.

Apply It! ※

When read-only text appears on the Web page, the user can select it. The user can then copy the text and paste it into another application. However, although disabled text appears on the Web page, the user cannot select it. This prevents the user from easily copying the text to another application.

Caution! ※

You can use the disabled and readonly attributes with other form items, such as checkboxes, but they may not work properly. For example, if you mark a number of checkboxes as disabled, the user can still select the checkboxes on the form, but the Web browser does not submit the checkbox information along with the rest of the form data.

DIFFICULTY LEVEL

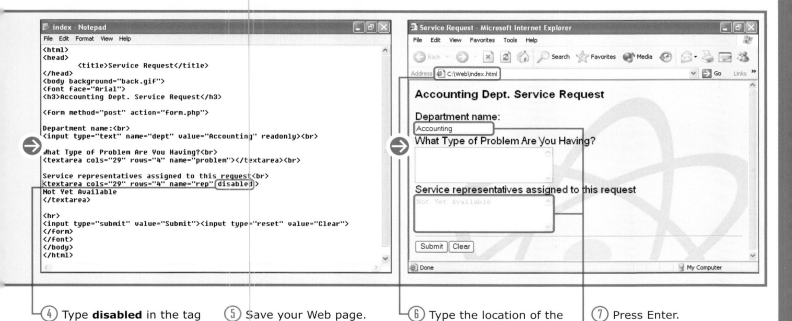

④ Type **disabled** in the tag for the text area.

⑤ Save your Web page.

⑥ Type the location of the Web page in your Web browser address bar.

⑦ Press Enter.

○ The unchangeable text appears in the form fields.

HIDE DATA
in forms

You can include form data that the user cannot see. This allows you to include your own data in forms along with the data the user enters. The Web browser recognizes the hidden data as if the user had typed it in along with the data in the non-hidden form fields. The Web browser then submits both the hidden and non-hidden data to the program or script that processes the form data. Users cannot change hidden form data, as the data does not appear when the Web browser displays the form.

You can use the input tag with a type value of hidden to create hidden data. The name attribute specifies the name you want to use to identify the data, while the value attribute contains the value of the hidden field. You can have an unlimited number of hidden fields in a form.

As with any field data on a form, the script or program that processes the form data must be able to use it. If a script or program does not require the hidden data, it ignores the data.

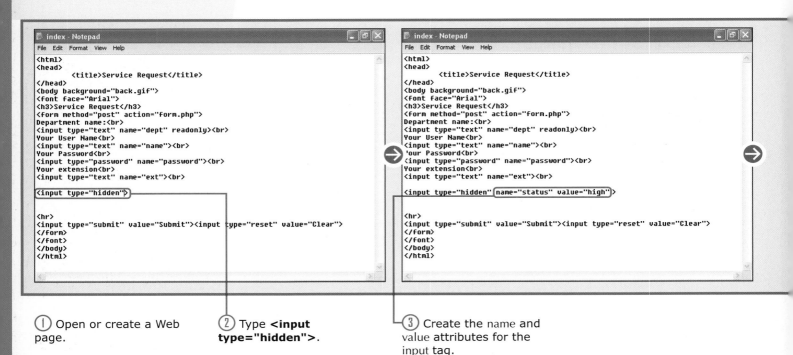

```
index - Notepad
File  Edit  Format  View  Help
<html>
<head>
        <title>Service Request</title>
</head>
<body background="back.gif">
<font face="Arial">
<h3>Service Request</h3>
<form method="post" action="form.php">
Department name:<br>
<input type="text" name="dept" readonly><br>
Your User Name<br>
<input type="text" name="name"><br>
Your Password<br>
<input type="password" name="password"><br>
Your extension<br>
<input type="text" name="ext"><br>

<input type="hidden">

<hr>
<input type="submit" value="Submit"><input type="reset" value="Clear">
</form>
</font>
</body>
</html>
```

```
index - Notepad
File  Edit  Format  View  Help
<html>
<head>
        <title>Service Request</title>
</head>
<body background="back.gif">
<font face="Arial">
<h3>Service Request</h3>
<form method="post" action="form.php">
Department name:<br>
<input type="text" name="dept" readonly><br>
Your User Name<br>
<input type="text" name="name"><br>
Your Password<br>
<input type="password" name="password"><br>
Your extension<br>
<input type="text" name="ext"><br>

<input type="hidden" name="status" value="high">

<hr>
<input type="submit" value="Submit"><input type="reset" value="Clear">
</form>
</font>
</body>
</html>
```

① Open or create a Web page.

② Type **<input type="hidden">**.

③ Create the name and value attributes for the input tag.

#59

DIFFICULTY LEVEL

Caution! ☀

Although it is hidden
from users, do not place
sensitive data in the hidden fields
of a form; they can easily view the
source HTML code of the Web page.

Apply It! ☀

Hidden data is used with multiple forms going
to one script. The form can use hidden data to
identify itself to the script that processes the data.
This allows you to use one script to process the
information submitted using many different forms.

Did You Know? ☀

When a program or script receives data
from a form, it cannot tell the difference
between user-typed and hidden-field-
generated information. If you create your own
scripts to process form data, you do not have to
do anything special to process hidden data.

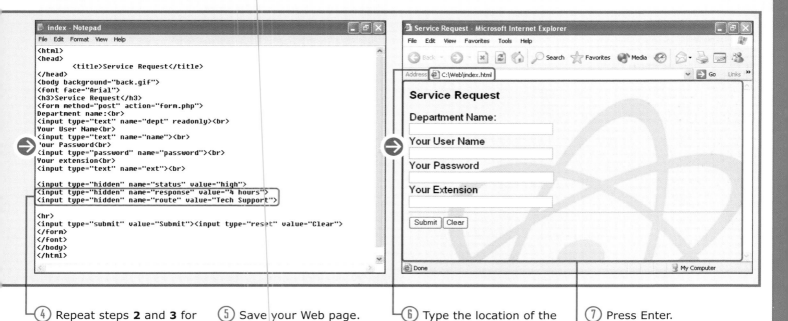

④ Repeat steps **2** and **3** for each hidden field you want to include in the form.

⑤ Save your Web page.

⑥ Type the location of the Web page in your Web browser address bar.

⑦ Press Enter.

○ The form appears without the hidden fields.

Add flair with
COLORED TEXT BOXES

You can change the appearance of the text boxes in your form to improve the look of your Web page or to make the information in the form easier to read. To change the appearance of a text box, you can use the style attribute with a value that contains different style properties.

The background-color property determines the color of the text box itself, while the color property determines the color of the text you type into the text box.

You can also add a colored border around a text box using the border property followed by a border size, color, and border style. For example, to create a border that consists of a thin line, you can use the solid border style.

As with all properties that you specify with the style attribute, the styles may not appear the way you intend when you view the Web page with an older Web browser.

① Open or create a Web page.

② Type **style="background-color: ?;"**, replacing ? with the name of the background color you want.

③ Type **border: ?px solid #;**, replacing ? with the border thickness and # with the border color.

#60

DIFFICULTY LEVEL

Caution! ※

When you choose colors for text boxes, you should pick contrasting colors for the background and the font. Some color combinations can make your text very hard to read, especially when you view them on the screen of a laptop computer.

Apply It! ※

You can apply style information to all the form elements that start with an input tag by creating a style block called input and placing it in the head section of the HTML code. Any style you specify applies to all input tag elements, including checkboxes and submit buttons. For example:

```
<style>
input { border:solid 2px blue; }
</style>
```

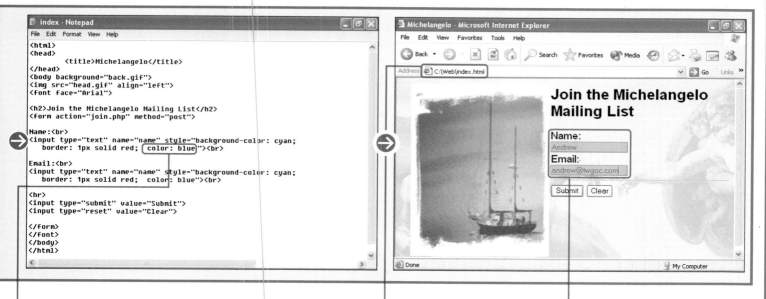

④ Type **color: ?**, replacing ? with the name of the text color you want.

⑤ Save your Web page.

⑥ Type the location of the Web page in your Web browser address bar.

⑦ Press Enter.

⑧ Type some text in the form fields.

○ The text and the text field backgrounds appear in different colors.

Create a
DEFAULT INSERTION
POINT LOCATION

You can make an insertion point appear in a specific field in a form when the form loads in a Web browser. When a user starts to type, the text appears in the form field that contains the insertion point.

You should set the form's focus to the most important field in the form. For example, if a form requires a username and password before proceeding, you can set the form's focus to these fields.

You can set the form's focus by using the onLoad event with the body tag. When the Web browser loads the page that contains the form, the JavaScript code executes, setting the focus to the form field that you specify.

You must add the name attribute to the input tag for the field that you want as your focus, as well as the form tag of the form that contains the input tag. The JavaScript code uses the name of the input tag and form to identify where it should place the focus.

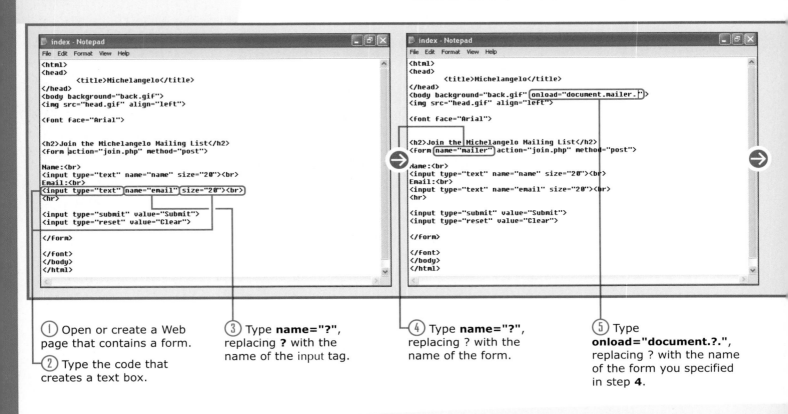

① Open or create a Web page that contains a form.

② Type the code that creates a text box.

③ Type **name="?"**, replacing **?** with the name of the input tag.

④ Type **name="?"**, replacing ? with the name of the form.

⑤ Type **onload="document.?."**, replacing ? with the name of the form you specified in step **4**.

Did You Know? ☀

Most search engines on the Internet set the focus to the form field where you type the search terms you want to locate. This makes the search engine easier to use.

Did You Know? ☀

If the insertion point is not in a field when a Web page loads, users must either click the mouse in the field, or press the tab key on the keyboard to move the insertion point to the field in which they want to type.

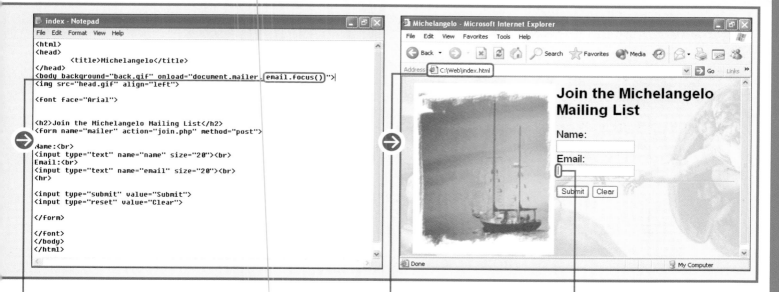

⑥ Type **?.focus()**, replacing ? with the name of the input tag you specified in step **3**.

⑦ Save your Web page.

⑧ Type the location of the Web page in your Web browser address bar.

⑨ Press Enter.

○ The insertion point appears in the form field you specified.

CHAPTER 7

Better Organize Your Data with Lists

Lists allow you to display a collection of items such as an index, a set of instructions, or a glossary. They primarily consist of text, such as a list of links, with usually no more than one or two lines of text per item.

You create a list using a descriptive tag to specify the type of list. The three types of lists are *definition*, *ordered*, and *unordered*. A list tag precedes each item in the list. List items typically appear indented, and preceded by a bullet.

A typical definition list is a list of single terms, each containing a few lines of text that explain the definition term. A glossary is a good example of the type of information you can use in a definition list.

An ordered list numbers all the items in ascending order. That is, the first item in the list starts with a number or letter, and the following items are labeled with a number or letter that is higher than the preceding item. Ordered lists are ideal for numbering items, such as the steps in a series of instructions, or to act as a counter when you display an inventory of items.

For unordered lists, the sequence in which items appear is not important, for example, a list of links to other Web pages or the members of a committee. You indent items in an unordered list and precede them with a bullet.

TOP 100

<td>
<tbody> <thead> <tr>
<table>

REVERSE A DEFINITION LIST

You can reverse a definition list so that it reads from right-to-left instead of from left-to-right. Definition lists are great to create glossaries, indexes, or even a menu of links. A reversed definition list aligns to the right side of a Web page, with the definition terms right aligning to the first term in the list.

A definition list consists of one or many terms. Each term is followed by a definition, which is slightly indented and appears on a line underneath the term.

The dt tag specifies a definition term. The dd tag specifies the definition and should immediately follow the associated dt tag. You must enclose the complete list in a definition list tag, dl.

To reverse a definition list, you specify the dir attribute for the dl tag. A value of ltr causes the list to appear from left to right, while a value of rtl causes the list to appear from right to left. Although not all Web browsers support the dir attribute, Internet Explorer supports it.

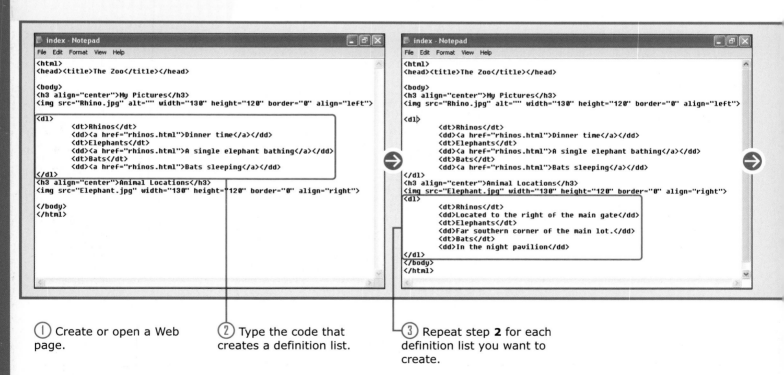

① Create or open a Web page.

② Type the code that creates a definition list.

③ Repeat step **2** for each definition list you want to create.

#62

DIFFICULTY LEVEL

Apply It!

If the number of definitions in a definition list is quite large, and the list consumes too much space on the Web page, you can compact the definition list to remove some of the space between the definitions, although not all browsers support this feature. To compact the definition list, add the attribute compact to the dl tag, for example:

`<dl compact dir="rtl">`

Did You Know?

In most cases you can safely ignore the closing dt and dd tags in a definition list. The Web browser still correctly displays the list even if you omit these tags.

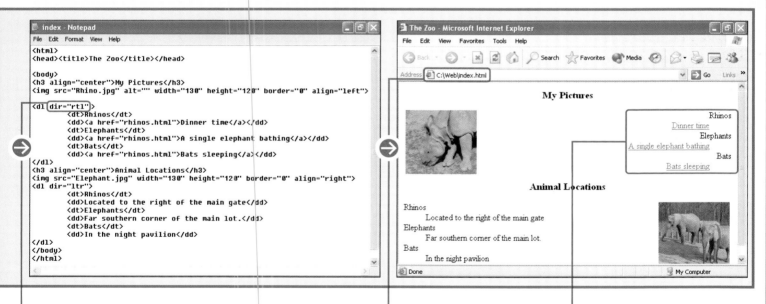

④ Type **dir="?"**, replacing ? with the value that determines how the list appears.

⑤ Save your Web page.

⑥ Type the location of the Web page in your Web browser address bar.

⑦ Press Enter.

○ The Web page displays with the list in reverse order.

Using lists to
INDENT IMAGES AND TEXT

You can use lists to indent items, such as text and images, on a Web page. This is handy when you want all the indented items to align. If you use multiple spaces to indent, the spaces reduce to only one space when the Web page displays.

HTML includes a number of tags that create lists. When you create a list, the items indent in order to make the list more readable. Lists normally require two tags, the list tag and the list item tag li.

However, you can use the list tag without the list item tag. When you do this, anything inside the list tag indents, as the Web browser is expecting a list item.

You can use the list tag ul to indent items. You should enclose desired text in the paragraph tag p, so that the Web browser knows which text you want to indent. Any image tags that you place between list tags also indent.

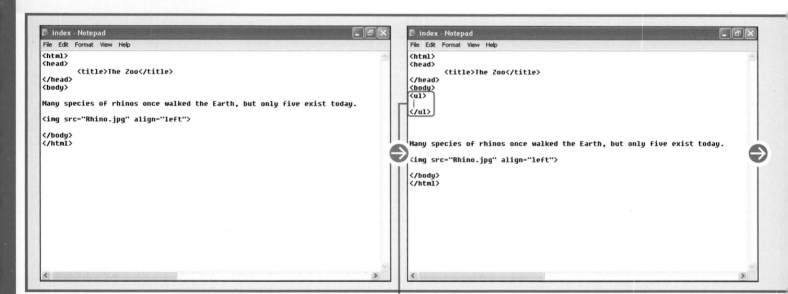

① Create or open a Web page.

② Type the opening and closing list tags.

Apply It! ☀

You can also use list tags to indent tables, links, or headings, or any other items on a Web page.

Caution! ☀

When displaying items, lists use bullets or numbering. Unless you use the list item tag li within the list tag, the bullets do not appear. There is no way to display list bullets beside items such as text or images when you are indenting them using only the list tag.

Did You Know? ☀

Although not all Web browsers support the compact attribute, you can try to add it to the list tag, to reduce the height of a list, for example:

```
<ul compact>
```

DIFFICULTY LEVEL

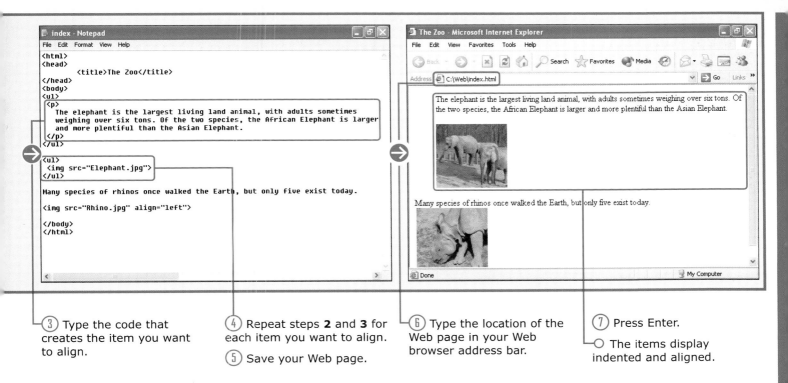

Ⓝ **index - Notepad**

File Edit Format View Help

```
<html>
<head>
        <title>The Zoo</title>
</head>
<body>
<ul>
<p>
    The elephant is the largest living land animal, with adults sometimes
    weighing over six tons. Of the two species, the African Elephant is larger
    and more plentiful than the Asian Elephant.
</p>
</ul>

<ul>
  <img src="Elephant.jpg">
</ul>

Many species of rhinos once walked the Earth, but only five exist today.

<img src="Rhino.jpg" align="left">

</body>
</html>
```

Ⓝ **The Zoo - Microsoft Internet Explorer**

File Edit View Favorites Tools Help

Back · ✕ ⟳ ⌂ Search Favorites Media

Address C:\Web\index.html Go Links

The elephant is the largest living land animal, with adults sometimes weighing over six tons. Of the two species, the African Elephant is larger and more plentiful than the Asian Elephant.

Many species of rhinos once walked the Earth, but only five exist today.

Done My Computer

③ Type the code that creates the item you want to align.

④ Repeat steps **2** and **3** for each item you want to align.

⑤ Save your Web page.

⑥ Type the location of the Web page in your Web browser address bar.

⑦ Press Enter.

○ The items display indented and aligned.

Organize data with
NESTED LISTS

You can place a list within another list to better present and organize data on your Web page. For example, you can use nested lists to display a large list of Web links.

Lists consist of list items, each preceded by the list item tag li, which are in turn all enclosed in a list tag. You can make lists unordered, using the ul tag, or ordered, using the ol tag.

To create a sub list, you can place another list after a list item in the primary list. The items in the sub

list become secondary items of the list item after which the sub list appears.

When you nest one unordered list within another unordered list, the bullet type for the primary list is different from the bullet type for the sub list. In most cases, the Web browser uses a solid circle as the first bullet and an outlined circle for the second bullet. When you use ordered lists, the bullet type is the same for each list.

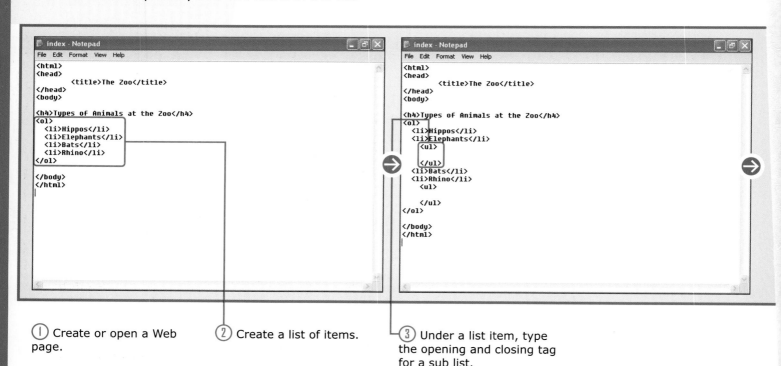

① Create or open a Web page.

② Create a list of items.

③ Under a list item, type the opening and closing tag for a sub list.

Caution! ※

You can continually nest links
to add sub lists. While there is no
limit to the amount of sub lists you can
use, having too many levels of lists can
make your information harder to read.

Apply It! ※

You can set the type of bullet that appears in an
unordered list by adding the type attribute with a value
that represents the bullet type.

Unordered Bullet Types	
Type	*Description*
disc	A small, solid circle
square	A solid square
circle	A simple (hollow) circle

DIFFICULTY LEVEL

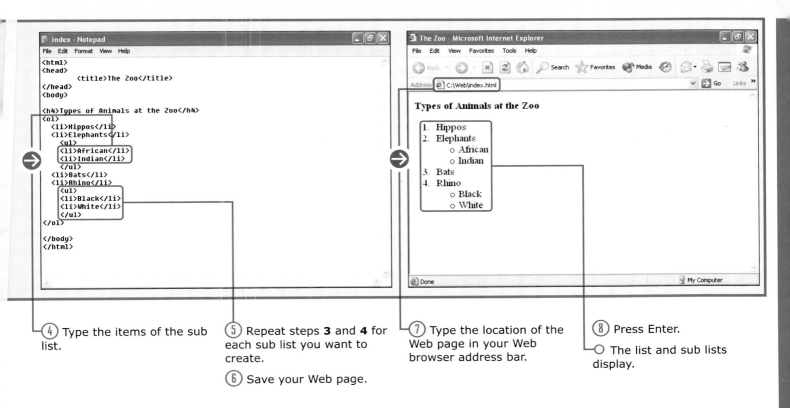

④ Type the items of the sub list.

⑤ Repeat steps **3** and **4** for each sub list you want to create.

⑥ Save your Web page.

⑦ Type the location of the Web page in your Web browser address bar.

⑧ Press Enter.

○ The list and sub lists display.

You can use images as bullets in your list to improve the list's appearance. By default, lists use small, solid circles for bullets. You can change the bullet style, but only to either a simple (hollow) circle or square.

However, you can also use an image as a bullet in your list. For example, you can create a bullet in the shape of a hyphen, with which you can then precede each list item. You insert the image file as a bullet into the list prior to each list item, using the image tag img.

To eliminate the bullets that you create using the list item tag li, you must eliminate the li tag from the list. This means that you must follow each item on the list with a break tag br, so that the next item appears on a new line.

In some cases the image you use may appear too close to the text. You can add space by using the hspace attribute of the img tag to insert horizontal space on either side of the image.

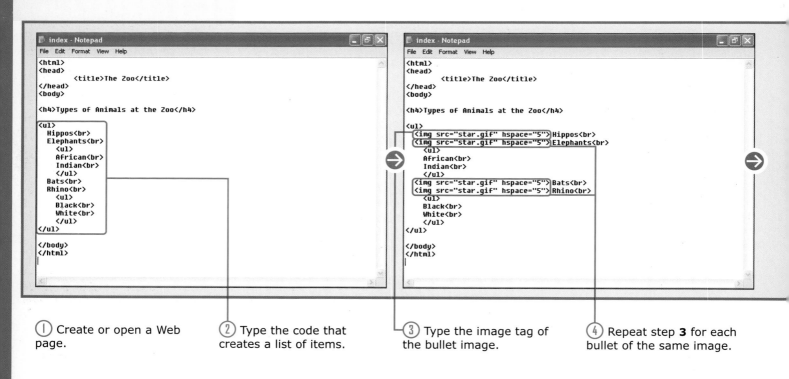

① Create or open a Web page.

② Type the code that creates a list of items.

③ Type the image tag of the bullet image.

④ Repeat step **3** for each bullet of the same image.

Apply It! ※

When you create an image for use as a bullet in your image-editing software, keep in mind that the size of the text next to the bullet may be a different size, depending on the user's text preferences. This may mean that the bullet you create may appear too high or too low when you place it with different-sized text.

DIFFICULTY LEVEL

Did You Know? ※

A Web browser only downloads an image once, and then redisplays the image if it uses that same image again. This means that even if you use an image as a bullet many times in your Web page, the Web browser still only downloads it once, speeding up the display of your Web pages.

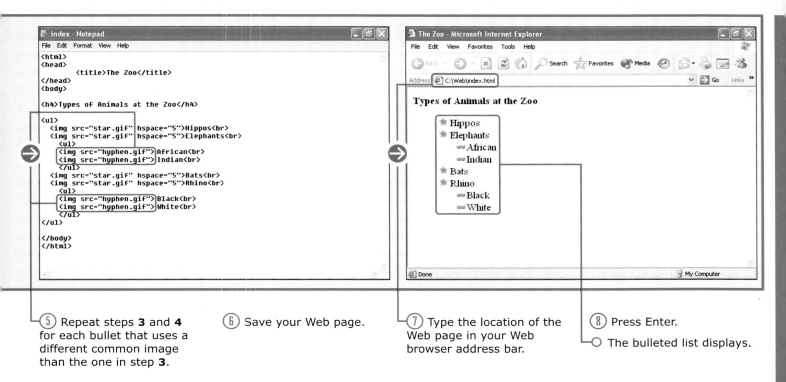

⑤ Repeat steps **3** and **4** for each bullet that uses a different common image than the one in step **3**.

⑥ Save your Web page.

⑦ Type the location of the Web page in your Web browser address bar.

⑧ Press Enter.

○ The bulleted list displays.

UNIQUE LIST SYMBOLS

One of the major limitations in working with HTML lists is the limited number of bullet types available for use. However, you can use styles to increase the number of available bullet types. This allows you to create bullets without having to create images.

You can use styles with many HTML elements, including lists. You can apply styles to list items by adding a style attribute to the list tag that encloses the list items. You can also apply a list style to ordered or unordered lists.

The list-style-type property defines the type of bullet, if any, that you want to use for the list items. You must separate the value and the list-style-type property with a colon.

If you are using nested style sheets and want to apply a style to all the lists in the collection, you must use a style tag for each list tag in the collection. See task #64 for more on nested lists. Internet Explorer supports the style attribute for bullets.

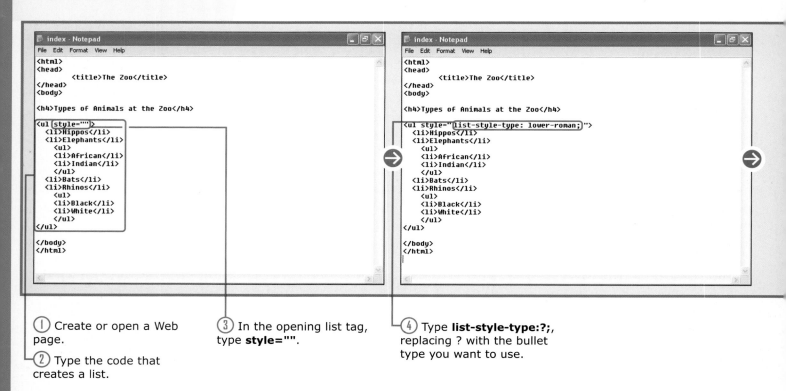

① Create or open a Web page.

② Type the code that creates a list.

③ In the opening list tag, type **style=""**.

④ Type **list-style-type:?;**, replacing ? with the bullet type you want to use.

Customize It!

You can use many values for the list-style-type property of the style attribute when you use it in a list tag.

List Bullet Type	
Type	*Description*
disc	A small, solid circle
circle	A small, outline circle
square	A solid, square block
decimal	A period
lower-roman	Roman numerals in lower case
upper-roman	Roman numerals in upper case
lower-alpha	Alphabetical, lower case
upper-alpha	Alphabetical, upper case
none	No bullets

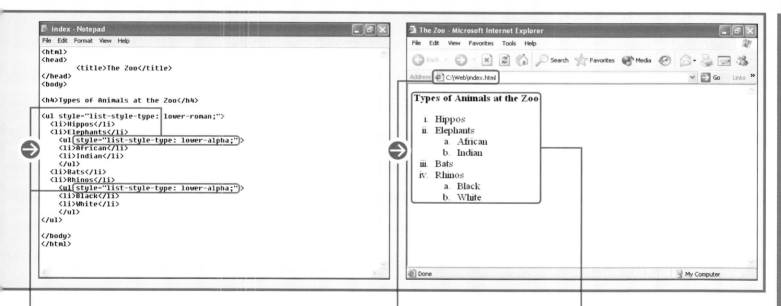

```
index - Notepad
File  Edit  Format  View  Help
<html>
<head>
        <title>The Zoo</title>
</head>
<body>

<h4>Types of Animals at the Zoo</h4>

<ul style="list-style-type: lower-roman;">
  <li>Hippos</li>
  <li>Elephants</li>
    <ul style="list-style-type: lower-alpha;">
    <li>African</li>
    <li>Indian</li>
    </ul>
  <li>Bats</li>
  <li>Rhinos</li>
    <ul style="list-style-type: lower-alpha;">
    <li>Black</li>
    <li>White</li>
    </ul>
</ul>

</body>
</html>
```

The Zoo - Microsoft Internet Explorer

Address C:\Web\index.html

Types of Animals at the Zoo

 i. Hippos
 ii. Elephants
        a. African
        b. Indian
 iii. Bats
 iv. Rhinos
        a. Black
        b. White

⑤ Repeat steps **3** and **4** for each bullet type you want to use.

⑥ Save your Web page.

⑦ Type the location of the Web page in your Web browser address bar.

⑧ Press Enter.

○ The list with the bullets appears.

CHAPTER 8

Arrange Your Objects Using Tables

You can use tables to organize data and information on a Web page. Tables are extremely useful for displaying columnar data such as information from a spreadsheet application.

You can place information into a table using table data cells. A table can consist of one or many individual table data cells, where each cell may or may not contain information. Tables consist of rows of cells, and the number of table cells in a row can vary within the same table. For example, you can have a row of ten data cells, preceded by a row that consists of only one data cell. The number of data cells can also vary by column. Enlarging table cells to straddle multiple rows or columns is called *spanning*.

As well as displaying numerical data, tables can also organize the layout of a Web page. You can place any kind of Web page element into a table cell, including an image, video, or a paragraph of text. Each table, and indeed each column, row, and data cell, can have its own unique attributes that affect the appearance and layout of items in the table. For example, you can control both the color and the alignment of items in a data cell. The ability to control the size, appearance, and layout of information within a table makes it easier to organize Web page data than if you were to simply place the information on a Web page.

TOP 100

<td>
<tbody> <thead> <tr>
<table>

Highlight information by
CHANGING TABLE COLORS

You can change the colors of the borders and background of a table to highlight important information.

The borders of a table consist of two parts, a light section and a dark section. The light and dark sections of the border work together to produce a table with a three-dimensional effect. You can individually specify the colors that you want to apply to the light and dark sections of the border.

The light section of the border consists of the left and top borders of the complete table, while the

dark section of the border consists of the right and bottom borders. The light and dark sections reverse for cell borders inside the table.

You can specify the border colors using the bordercolorlight and bordercolordark attributes of the table tag.

Apart from the border color, you can also assign a color to the background of the table. This color should contrast with the information in the table to make the information easy to read.

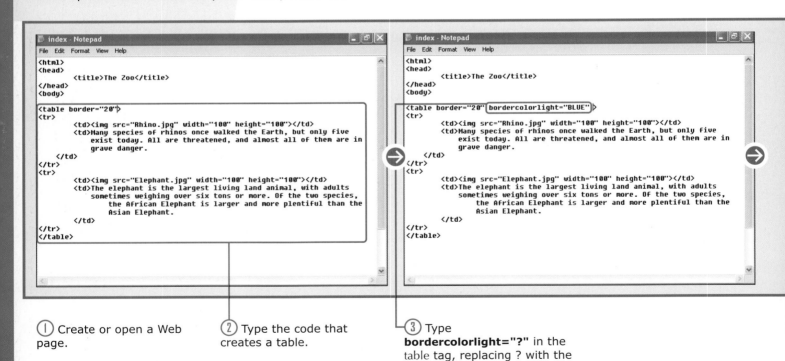

① Create or open a Web page.

② Type the code that creates a table.

③ Type **bordercolorlight="?"** in the table tag, replacing ? with the color you want to assign to the light border color.

Apply It

If you do not want to specify different colors for the light and dark sections of the table border, you can simply specify a single color that applies to both the light and dark sections of the border. You can do this by using the border color attribute without using the bordercolorlight and bordercolordark attributes. For example:

```
<table border="20" border color="YELLOW">
```

Apply It

You can also utilize the bordercolorlight and bordercolordark attributes on individual cells in a table by using the attributes in the td tag. The attribute values in a td tag override the attributes in the table tag. For example:

```
<td bordercolorlight="GREY" bordercolordark="BLUE">
```

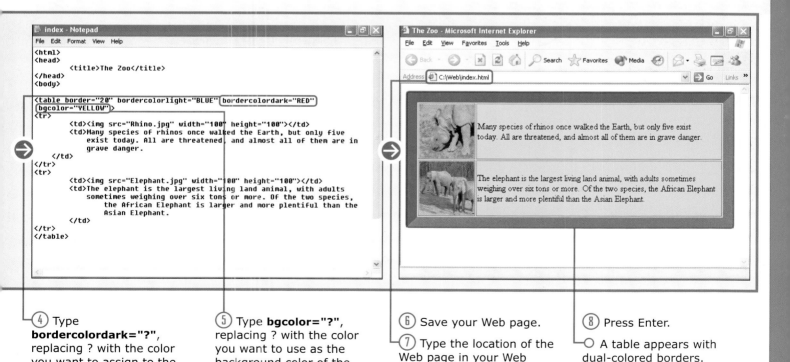

④ Type **bordercolordark="?"**, replacing ? with the color you want to assign to the dark border color.

⑤ Type **bgcolor="?"**, replacing ? with the color you want to use as the background color of the table.

⑥ Save your Web page.

⑦ Type the location of the Web page in your Web browser address bar.

⑧ Press Enter.

○ A table appears with dual-colored borders.

	JAN	FEB	MAR
Boston	$150K	$175K	$214K
Chicago	$220K	$225K	$250K
Dallas	$370K	$352K	$354K
Memphis	$143K	$127K	$201K
Denver	$137K	$220K	$254K

Enhance a table with
BACKGROUND IMAGES

You can use images as backgrounds in tables to enhance the appearance of the tables on your Web page. Each table cell in a table can have a different background. You add a background image to a table cell by using the background attribute in the table data cell tag td.

If the table cell is larger than the background image, the image *tiles*, that is, the image repeats to fill the background of the cell.

If the image you use as a background is bigger than the table cell for which it is the background, the image is cropped to fit the table cell. The amount and type of the information that appears in the table cell determines the size of the cell.

You can use images that are in GIF or JPG file format. If you use images as table cell backgrounds, you should ensure that the contents of the cell contrast with the background images so that a user can easily read them.

```
index - Notepad
File Edit Format View Help
<html>
<head>
<title>The Zoo</title>
</head>
<body>

  <table width="40%">
    <tr>
      <td><font color="YELLOW"><strong>Many
      species of rhinos once walked the Earth, but only five exist
      today. All are threatened, and almost all of them are in grave
      danger.</strong></font>
      </td>
    </tr>
    <tr>
      <td><font color="WHITE"><strong>The
      elephant is the largest living land animal, with adults
      sometimes weighing over six tons or more. Of the two species,
      the African Elephant is larger and more plentiful than the
      Asian Elephant.</strong></font>
      </td>
    </tr>
  </table>

</body>
</html>
```

```
index - Notepad
File Edit Format View Help
<html>
<head>
<title>The Zoo</title>
</head>
<body>

  <table width="40%">
    <tr>
      <td background="Rhino.jpg"><font color="YELLOW"><strong>Many
      species of rhinos once walked the Earth, but only five exist
      today. All are threatened, and almost all of them are in grave
      danger.</strong></font>
      </td>
    </tr>
    <tr>
      <td><font color="WHITE"><strong>The
      elephant is the largest living land animal, with adults
      sometimes weighing over six tons or more. Of the two species,
      the African Elephant is larger and more plentiful than the
      Asian Elephant.</strong></font>
      </td>
    </tr>
  </table>

</body>
</html>
```

① Create or open a Web page.

② Type the code that adds a table to the Web page.

③ Type **background="?"**, in the td tag replacing ? with the name of the image you want to use as the cell background.

Apply It! ☀

If you prefer, you can use a single image as the background for the whole table instead of having images for individual cells. Use the background attribute of the table tab to specify the name of the background image you want to have as the table background. For example:

`<table width="40%" background="Rhino. jpg">`

DIFFICULTY LEVEL

Did You Know? ☀

The size of information in a table cell determines the size of the cell. However, you can adjust the table cell size by changing the size of the Web browser font, which changes the size of any text on a Web page, including the text placed in table cells.

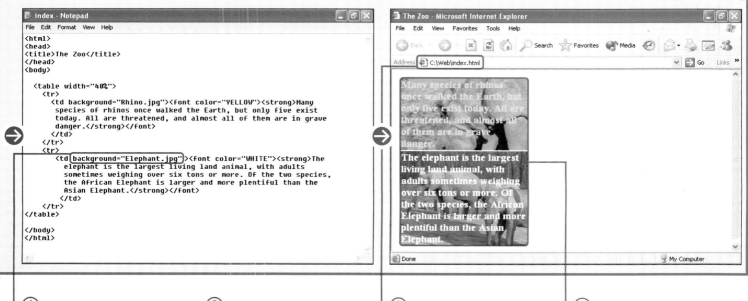

④ Repeat step **3** for each table cell background you want to add.

⑤ Save your Web page.

⑥ Type the location of the Web page in your Web browser address bar.

⑦ Press Enter.

○ The table cells display with their backgrounds.

SPECIFY TABLE SIZE
to control page layout

You can specify the dimensions of a table to control the layout of a Web page, regardless of the resolution at which the Web page displays.

One of the problems with designing Web sites is that the Web page designer has very little control over how the Web page appears at different resolutions. One way to control the layout of a Web page is to construct a table at a fixed size and then place the contents of the Web page in the table.

You can specify the dimensions of a table using the width and height attributes in the table tag. The values for these attributes determine the size of the table in pixels.

If the table size that you specify is smaller than what you need to display the content of the table, the dimensions of the table increase to accommodate all the data in the table.

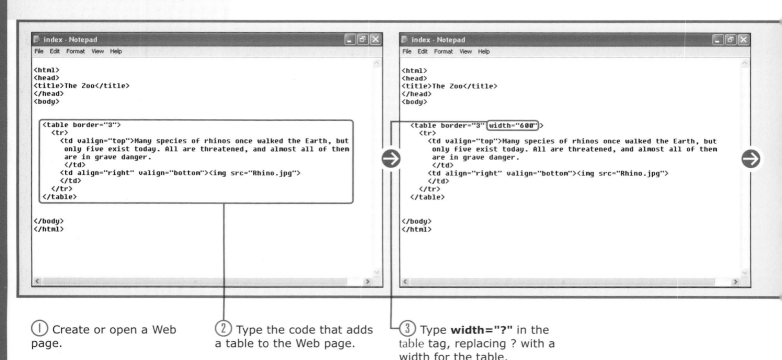

① Create or open a Web page.

② Type the code that adds a table to the Web page.

③ Type **width="?"** in the table tag, replacing ? with a width for the table.

Did You Know? ☀

The lowest monitor resolution commonly in use is 800 pixels wide by 600 pixels high. With allowances for window borders, scroll bars, and toolbars, the display area of a Web page is about 750 pixels wide by 450 pixels high. If you design your Web pages at this resolution and use a table to constrain the Web page, the Web page also looks similar when you view it at higher resolutions.

Apply It! ☀

Instead of specifying the table size in pixels, you can specify it as a percentage of the Web page window. For example, to create a table that spans halfway across the Web browser window from top to bottom, use:

```html
<table width="50%" height="100%">
```

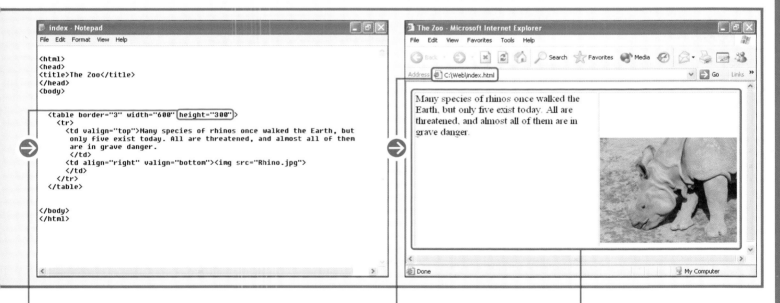

④ Type **height="?"** in the table tag, replacing ? with a height for the table.

⑤ Save your Web page.

⑥ Type the location of the Web page in your Web browser address bar.

⑦ Press Enter.

○ The table displays with the dimensions you specify.

ARRANGE ITEMS WITHIN TABLES
for creative layout

You can arrange items, such as text and images, within a table to control the layout of your Web page. For example, you can surround an item of text with a number of images if you arrange the items in a table.

You can ensure that items that you place in different table cells are next to each other by setting the border width of the table to 0. The cellpadding and cellmargin attributes dictate the distance between

neighboring cells and the internal margins of individual cells, respectively. You must set these attributes to 0 in order to place items next to each other.

You can align items vertically in a table cell by using the valign attribute of the td tag. Setting a valign attribute with a value of top places the item in a table cell at the top of the table cell. By default, items appear in the middle of the table cell.

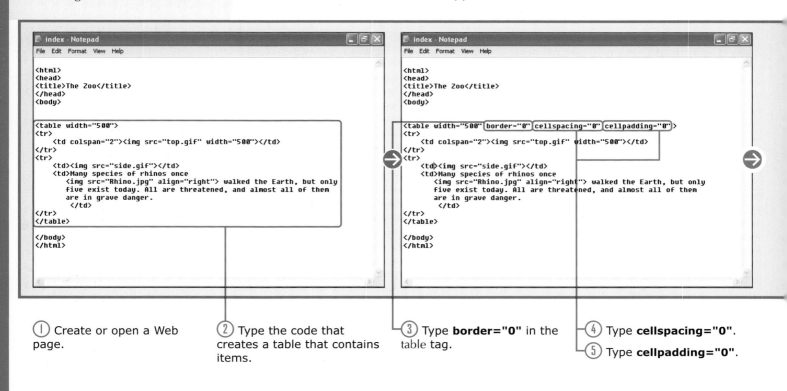

① Create or open a Web page.

② Type the code that creates a table that contains items.

③ Type **border="0"** in the table tag.

④ Type **cellspacing="0"**.

⑤ Type **cellpadding="0"**.

Did You Know? ※

You can align all items in a table cell to the left or the right using the align attribute of the td tag. The align="left" attribute places items at the left side of the table cell and is the default alignment for table cells, while align="right" places items on the right side of the table cell. To align all the data cells in a complete row in a table, use the align attribute. You should use the align attribute with the table row tag tr that encloses the td cells, which contain the aligned data.

#70

DIFFICULTY LEVEL

Apply It! ※

There are a number of values for the valign attribute that you can use to align items vertically in a table cell.

valign Attribute Values	
Value	*Purpose*
top	Aligns items with the top of the table cell.
bottom	Aligns items with the bottom of the table cell.
middle	Aligns items with the center of the table cell.
baseline	Aligns items with the bottom of the first line of text in adjoining table cells.

⑥ Type **valign="top"** in any td tag where you want to align items to the top of the cell.

⑦ Save your Web page.

⑧ Type the location of the Web page in your Web browser address bar.

⑨ Press Enter.

○ The items that you specify in the table align to the top of the table cells.

Organize data by
INSERTING TABLE HEADERS

You can use table headers to label and organize data in a table on your Web page.

There are two types of cells that you can use in a table. The most common is the table data cell. You can use it to store information such as text, images, and links. You can specify table data cells using the td tag. The other type of cell is the table header cell. A table header cell identifies information in a table. For example, if you have a table with one column of

data cells that you use to store calendar dates, you can place a table header cell at the top of the column containing the word **dates**.

You can use the th tag to place a table header cell in a table. The Web browser applies formatting, typically in bold font, to any text that you place in a table header cell. This allows you to use text you want to emphasize in your table without having to use separate font or text-formatting tags.

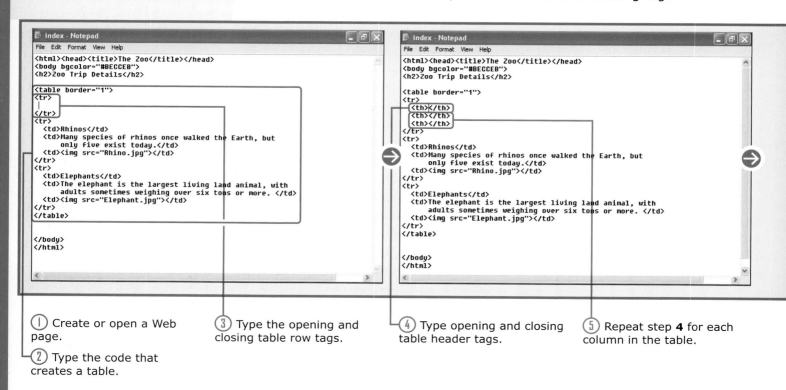

① Create or open a Web page.

② Type the code that creates a table.

③ Type the opening and closing table row tags.

④ Type opening and closing table header tags.

⑤ Repeat step **4** for each column in the table.

#71

DIFFICULTY LEVEL

Apply It! ※

You can use the rowspan and colspan attributes with your table header cells to span multiple rows or columns just like the td tag. For example, to create a table with a header cell that spans across two columns of table data cells, you can use the code below:

```
<table>
<tr><th colspan="2"></tr>
<tr><td></td><td></td></tr>
</table>
```

Did You Know? ※

Proper use of table headings can make it easier for search engines to analyze and categorize the information on your Web page.

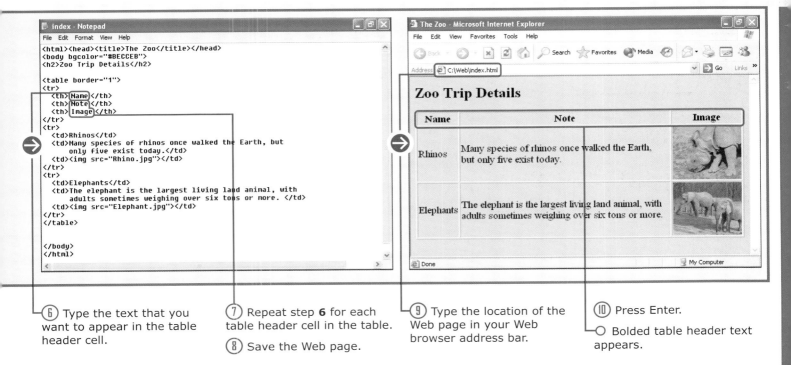

⑥ Type the text that you want to appear in the table header cell.

⑦ Repeat step **6** for each table header cell in the table.

⑧ Save the Web page.

⑨ Type the location of the Web page in your Web browser address bar.

⑩ Press Enter.

○ Bolded table header text appears.

Using a table to
CREATE AN IMAGE MAP

An image map uses parts of an image to represent links to other Web pages. Because image maps can be difficult to create, you can use a table to achieve a similar result.

To make an image map, you must first create an image in your image-editing program. You must then divide the image into sections, each of which represents a link. You can then place each section of the image into a different data cell in the table. Most operating systems come with image-editing

programs that divide images into sections. Complex and sophisticated images may require a more powerful image-editing program.

In order for the image sections to appear as one image, you must eliminate all extra space from the table. You can do this by setting the cellspacing attribute, which determines the distance between cells, and the cellpadding attribute, which determines margins in cells, to a value of 0. You must also set the border of the table to 0.

Once you align the images in a table, you can encapsulate them in an a tag to turn them into links.

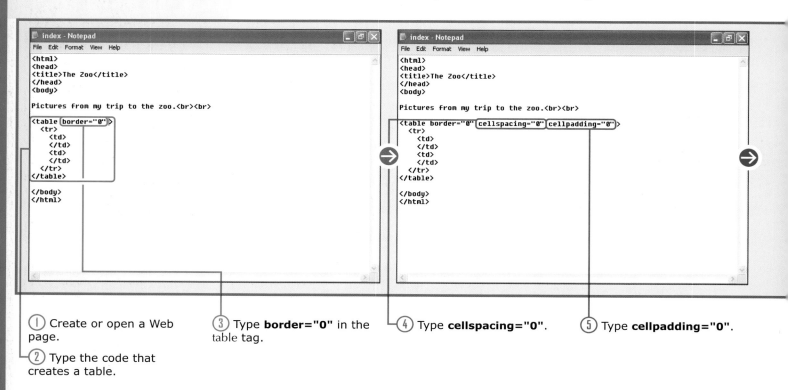

① Create or open a Web page.

② Type the code that creates a table.

③ Type **border="0"** in the table tag.

④ Type **cellspacing="0"**.

⑤ Type **cellpadding="0"**.

Customize It! ⁂

You can make the table that
you use to create an image map
as simple or as complex as you need
it to be. Not every image section has to
be a link, so you can combine regular
images and images used as links to create
sophisticated image maps.

#72

DIFFICULTY LEVEL

Caution! ⁂

When creating a table that you want to use as
an image map, you must ensure that no spaces
or text interfere with the layout of the table. If
your table does not look right, remove any
unnecessary whitespace, such as tabs, new lines,
and spaces, from the HTML code that makes up the
table.

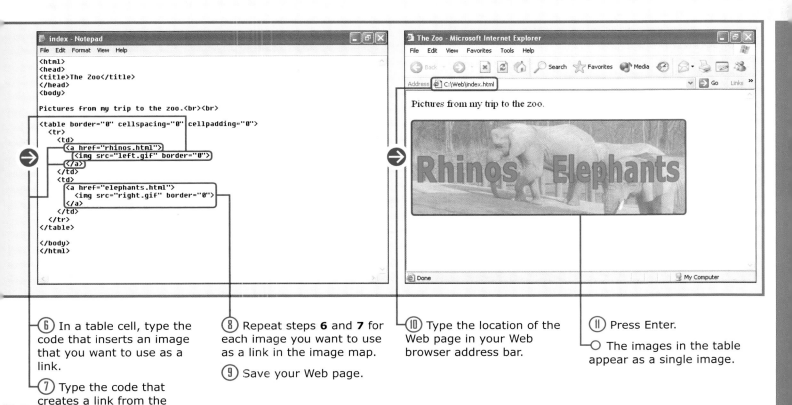

⑥ In a table cell, type the
code that inserts an image
that you want to use as a
link.

⑦ Type the code that
creates a link from the
image.

⑧ Repeat steps **6** and **7** for
each image you want to use
as a link in the image map.

⑨ Save your Web page.

⑩ Type the location of the
Web page in your Web
browser address bar.

⑪ Press Enter.

○ The images in the table
appear as a single image.

Using Two Tables to CREATE BORDERS AROUND OBJECTS

While you can apply borders to some objects, such as images, other objects, such as text, have no easy way to apply a border. You can use a combination of two tables to draw a border around any object on a Web page.

To create a border around an object, you can create a table containing a fixed, solid background and a single cell. You can place another table in the cell with a background color that matches the Web page background. If the interior table is smaller than the

table that contains it, a border appears around any object that you place in the table. You can use the cellpadding attribute of the first table to specify a value for the width of the colored border.

You can add any Web page object to the table cell of the inner table. The object then has a border drawn around it. You can also add multiple items, such as a table, text, and an image to the table cell, to have a border drawn around all of the objects.

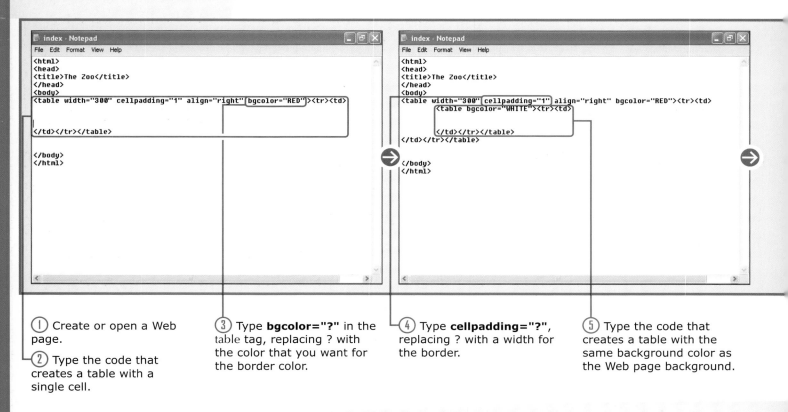

① Create or open a Web page.

② Type the code that creates a table with a single cell.

③ Type **bgcolor="?"** in the table tag, replacing ? with the color that you want for the border color.

④ Type **cellpadding="?"**, replacing ? with a width for the border.

⑤ Type the code that creates a table with the same background color as the Web page background.

DIFFICULTY LEVEL

Apply It! ✳

You can create more elaborate borders by nesting multiple tables within a table cell. As long as the background color of each subsequent table is different, a new border is drawn for each table.

Apply It! ✳

The table tag itself has a border attribute, which you can use to draw three-dimensional borders around a table. You can add these borders to the inner table to produce a colored, three-dimensional border around an object.

Apply It! ✳

To ensure that the inner table extends over the entire area of the table cell that contains it, you can add the width and height attributes to the inner table tag and set both values to 100%. For example:

```
<table bicolor="WHITE" width="100%" height="100%">
```

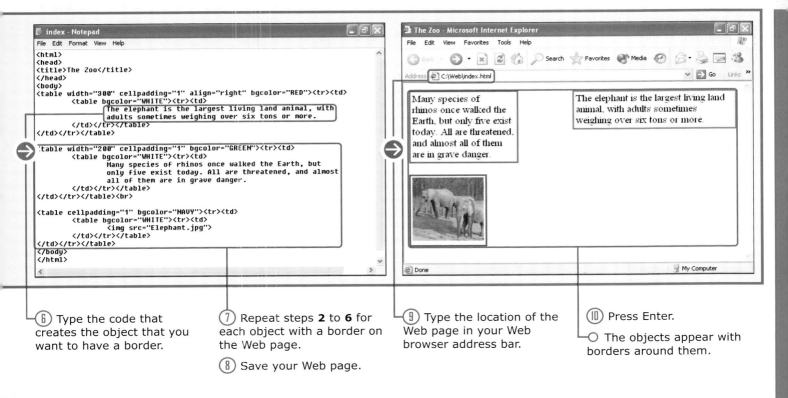

⑥ Type the code that creates the object that you want to have a border.

⑦ Repeat steps **2** to **6** for each object with a border on the Web page.

⑧ Save your Web page.

⑨ Type the location of the Web page in your Web browser address bar.

⑩ Press Enter.

○ The objects appear with borders around them.

	JAN	FEB	MAR
Boston	$150K	$175K	$214K
Chicago	$220K	$225K	$250K
Dallas	$370K	$352K	$354K
Memphis	$143K	$127K	$201K
Denver	$137K	$220K	$254K

Create DYNAMIC TABLE MENUS

You can use tables to create menus that dynamically change as a mouse pointer moves over the contents of the menus. Dynamic menus give your users visual feedback about the choices they make in your menus.

You can use a few lines of JavaScript code to dynamically change the background color of your table cells.

You can create a dynamic menu by placing a link within a table cell that has a background color. When the mouse pointer moves over the menu, the

JavaScript event onMouseOver sets the background of the table cell to a different color from the background color of the table. When the mouse pointer moves off a table cell, the onMouseOut event changes the color of the cell back to the original color.

You can insert the JavaScript code that controls the color of the cell background into the td tag of the table.

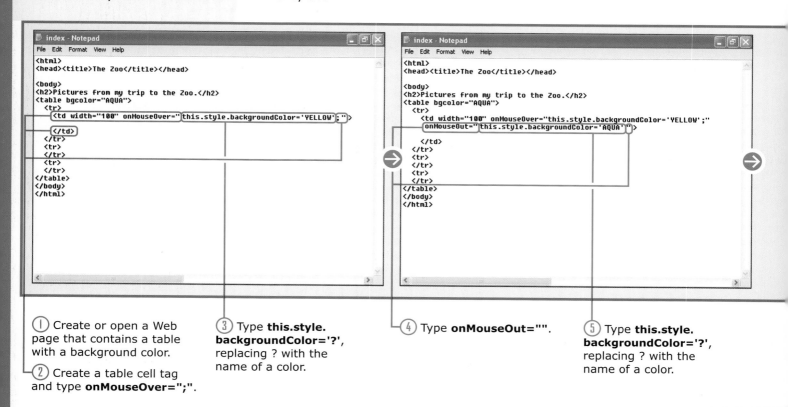

1 Create or open a Web page that contains a table with a background color.

2 Create a table cell tag and type **onMouseOver=";"**.

3 Type **this.style. backgroundColor='?'**, replacing ? with the name of a color.

4 Type **onMouseOut=""**.

5 Type **this.style. backgroundColor='?'**, replacing ? with the name of a color.

74

Caution! ※

By default, a text link appears in blue until you visit the link, at which point it appears purple. You should ensure that the colors that you choose for the table background and cells contrast with these colors so that your users can easily read the menu text.

Apply It! ※

When the mouse pointer moves off a table cell, the background color of the cell changes to that of the table. For a different effect, you can change the color of the cell to a different color. For example, to change the background color of a cell to black after the mouse pointer moves over it, change the color that you specify in the onMouseOut event to BLACK. For example:

```
onMouseOut="this.style.backgroundColor='BLACK'
```

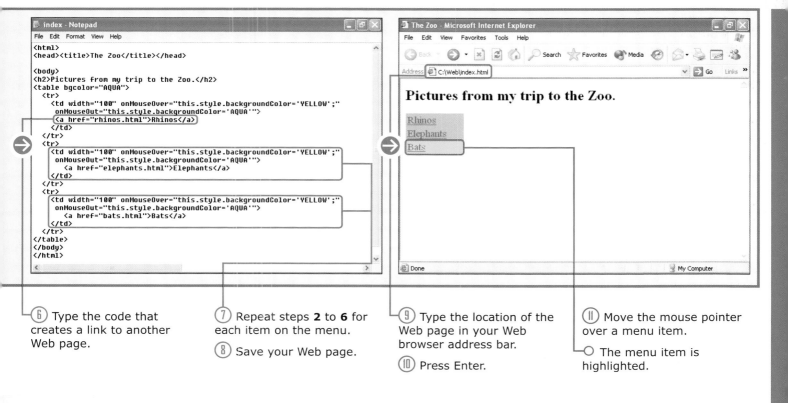

⑥ Type the code that creates a link to another Web page.

⑦ Repeat steps **2** to **6** for each item on the menu.

⑧ Save your Web page.

⑨ Type the location of the Web page in your Web browser address bar.

⑩ Press Enter.

⑪ Move the mouse pointer over a menu item.

○ The menu item is highlighted.

CHAPTER 9

Tap Your Browser's Hidden Power with JavaScript

JavaScript is responsible for many of the interactive and dynamic features on Web sites today. JavaScript code works within your HTML code to perform special processes. Almost all Web browsers currently in use can process JavaScript code. However, you should test your JavaScript code on as many Web browsers as possible to ensure that it is compatible.

JavaScript uses the same programming methods as most other programming languages, so if you are familiar with other programming languages, you should find JavaScript easy to use. JavaScript uses methods, or statements, to generate values and text as well as to perform functions. Methods consist of a method name, and one or more keywords separated by

periods, followed by a set of parentheses that may or may not contain arguments.

You can use the script tag to place JavaScript code anywhere in your HTML code, including the head section, the body, or even within individual tags.

Events associated with tags often access JavaScript code. You use events in the same way as tag attributes. For example, the onClick event processes any JavaScript code it contains when the user clicks on the item generated by the tag.

JavaScript can enhance the functionality of many Web page features such as links and mouse operation. You can also use it to provide additional information like message boxes, status messages, or simply the date and time.

TOP 100

You can add date and time information to your Web page to make it appear more dynamic. You can also customize the appearance of the date and time information. To do this, you must enclose the JavaScript code that generates the date and time within any HTML tag that applies to text, such as the font tag. When you view the Web page, the surrounding HTML tag applies to the date and time that the JavaScript code generates.

JavaScript accesses the date and time information using the Date property, and then displays this information with the document.write statement. The

document.write statement generates text that you want to insert in the HTML code of the Web page. You can use the document.write statement to produce additional text in combination with the date and time information. To use the document.write statement to display text, you can simply place the text within quotation marks. You can combine text with other items in the document.write statement by using the plus symbol.

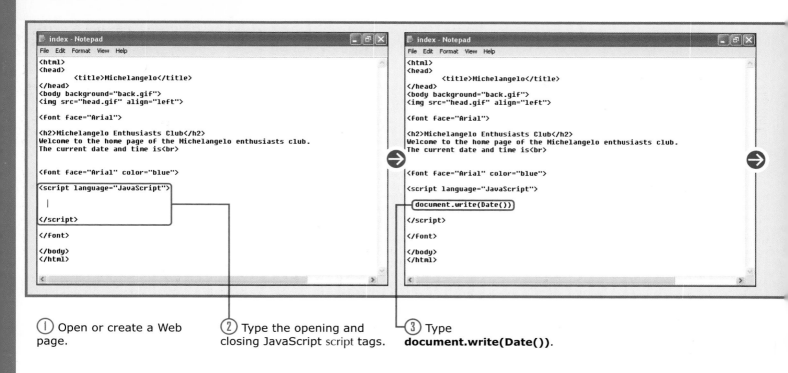

① Open or create a Web page.

② Type the opening and closing JavaScript script tags.

③ Type **document.write(Date())**.

DIFFICULTY LEVEL

Caution!

JavaScript gathers the date
and time information from the
computer of the user who is viewing
your Web page. This allows users to see
their local time, but it also means that if
their computer clock is set incorrectly, the
time on the Web page is also incorrect.
Because users from different time zones may
view your Web page, remember to avoid
references to your local time zone.

Did You Know?

When you use JavaScript to display the date and
time on a Web page, it only generates the date
and time when the Web page loads and does not
constantly update. To display the latest date and
time information after a Web page loads, you must
refresh the Web page.

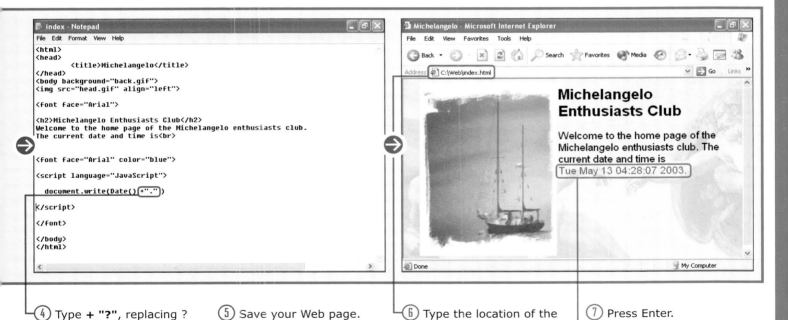

④ Type + "?", replacing ? with any text you want to display after the date and time.

⑤ Save your Web page.

⑥ Type the location of the Web page in your Web browser address bar.

⑦ Press Enter.

○ The date and time appear on the Web page.

NAVIGATION LINKS

You can create dynamic links on your Web pages that let users return to the Web page they were previously viewing. A back link displays the page the user was viewing prior to the Web page that contains the back link, regardless of what page it was.

You can create a navigation link that takes the user back to the previous page by using a standard link tag a. You must then use the hash symbol, #, as the address of the Web page to which you want to link.

You can add an onClick event to the link tag to allow the user to change the address of the Web page that

displays in the Web browser to the Web page that previously appeared. JavaScript uses the history.go statement to indicate the page in the history file that you want to display. For example, an argument of –1 for this statement takes the user back one page.

Using a link to the previous page is the same as clicking the Back button on the toolbar of the Web browser.

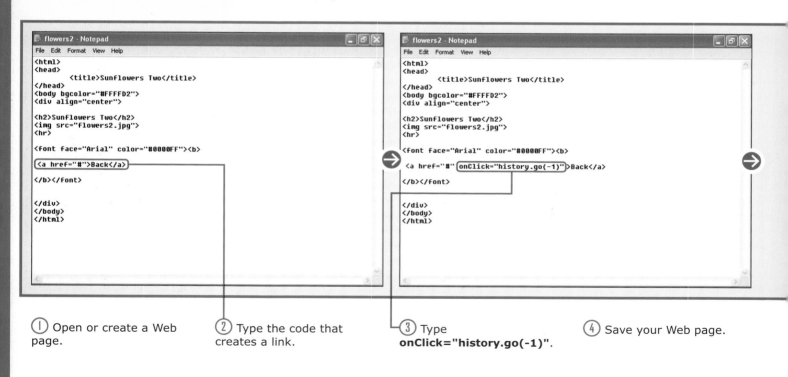

① Open or create a Web page.

② Type the code that creates a link.

③ Type **onClick="history.go(-1)"**.

④ Save your Web page.

DIFFICULTY LEVEL

Did You Know?

Every Web browser stores the history of the Web pages that a user has viewed in a cache. If a user clears this cache of files just prior to clicking a back link, the current Web page remains in the display window.

Apply It!

You can create a button instead of a text link by using the input tag:

```
<input type="button" value="Back"  onClick="history.go(-1)">
```

Did You Know?

It is best to place a back link on the sub pages of your Web site and not on the main page. If there is a back link on the main page and users select it, they return to the previous page they were viewing, which may not be a Web page from your site.

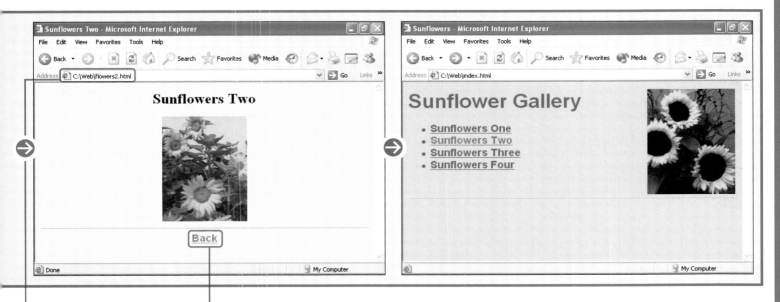

➎ Open or navigate to the Web page that contains the back link.

➏ Click the back link.

○ The previous Web page displays.

SHOW MESSAGES
in the status bar

At the bottom of the Web browser, a status bar displays information about Web pages and the status of the Web browser. For example, if a Web page contains an error, a message may appear in the status bar describing the error. You can place text into the status bar to provide more information about the Web pages you create.

There are two events that you can use when you want to display messages in the status bar. The onMouseOver event executes JavaScript code when the mouse pointer moves over an item. This code

displays a message in the status bar. The onMouseOut event executes JavaScript code when a user moves the mouse pointer off an item. This code removes the message from the status bar by simply writing an empty string of text that contains nothing in the status bar.

The window.status property contains the text you want to appear in the status bar. Assigning text to this JavaScript property causes the text to appear in the status bar.

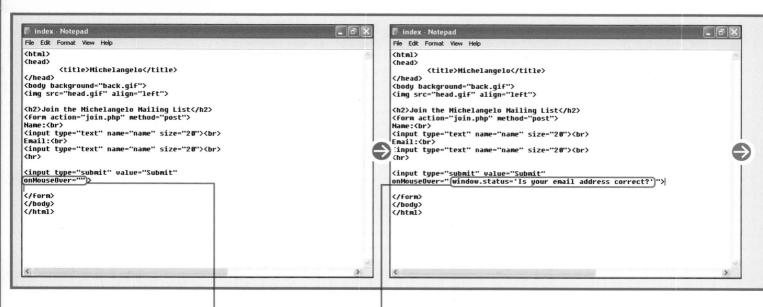

① Open or create a Web page.

② Type **onMouseOver=""** in the tag for which you want to create a status message.

③ Type **window.status='?'**, replacing ? with the text you want to appear in the status bar.

Apply It!

You should ensure that the width and height specifications for the pop-up window are large enough to display the complete Web page in the pop-up window. Many Web browsers open a pop-up window with no scrollbars, so if the page does not fully display, the user has no easy way of viewing all of the Web page in the pop-up window.

Apply It!

For each pop-up window, you specify the name of the window as the second argument of the window.open statement. If a user attempts to open a pop-up window that has the same name as the pop-up window that currently displays, the Web page displays in the existing pop-up window. The browser does not create a new pop-up window.

⑦ Type the location of the Web page in your Web browser address bar.

⑧ Press Enter.

⑨ Click the link to the pop-up window.

○ The pop-up window appears.

INCLUDE A CLOSE BUTTON
to a pop-up window

You can add a button to a Web page that allows a user to close the Web browser window in which the Web page displays. A Close button is a useful addition to a Web page that displays in a pop-up window. This is because some pop-up windows do not have toolbars. A Close button makes it more convenient for the user to close the pop-up window.

Clicking a Close button on a Web page is similar to clicking the close windows icon that you find in the top-right corner of most Web browser windows.

The window.close JavaScript statement tells the current Web browser window to close whenever the statement executes. You can use the onClick event to assign the window.close() statement to a button that you create with the button tag.

The text you use on the Close button should be clear, indicating that the window closes when a user clicks the button.

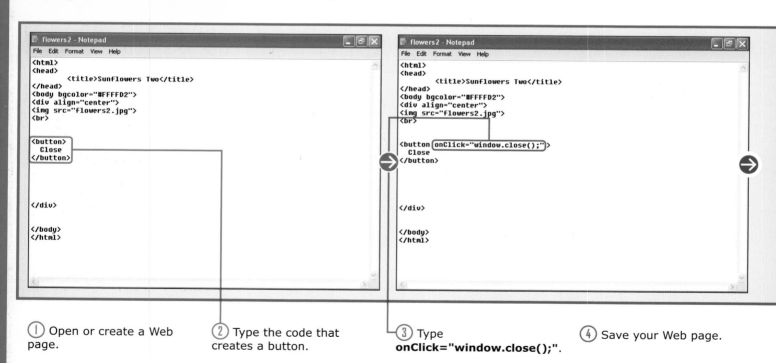

① Open or create a Web page.

② Type the code that creates a button.

③ Type **onClick="window.close();"**.

④ Save your Web page.

Apply It!

You do not have to use a button to close a Web browser window; you can also use the onClick event with another element, such as an image. For example:

`<img src="close.jpg" onClick="window.close();">`

Apply It!

You can ensure that a pop-up window closes no matter where the user clicks the pop-up window by assigning the onClick event that closes the window to the body tag of the Web page:

`<body onClick="window.close();">`

Caution!

You should only use a Close button on Web pages that open in pop-up windows. If you include a Close button on any other type of Web page, the user may accidentally shut down the Web browser when they click the Close button.

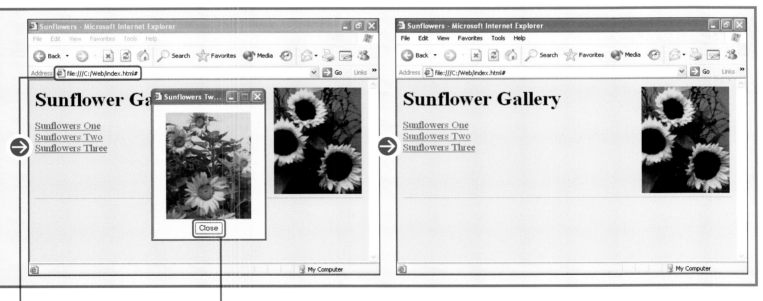

⑤ Open or navigate to the Web page that contains the Close button.

⑥ Click the Close button.

○ The Web page window closes.

Customize the
FEATURES OF A
POP-UP WINDOW

You can customize the features of a pop-up window. For example, you can choose to have a window display a toolbar. For more on creating pop-up windows, see task #78.

The window.open statement takes three arguments. The first two specify the name of the Web page you want to load in the new window and the name of the window, respectively. The third argument specifies the different features of the new window.

You can assign properties to control the different features of the window. For example, you can choose to display a scrollbar in the new window. If

the Web page is larger than the new window, a scrollbar allows the user to view the complete Web page. Each Web browser window can also have a status bar at the bottom of the window. You can use the status bar to provide information about the contents of the Web page. You can also add the toolbar at the top of a Web browser window. The toolbar is the main menu bar that contains the Back and Refresh buttons.

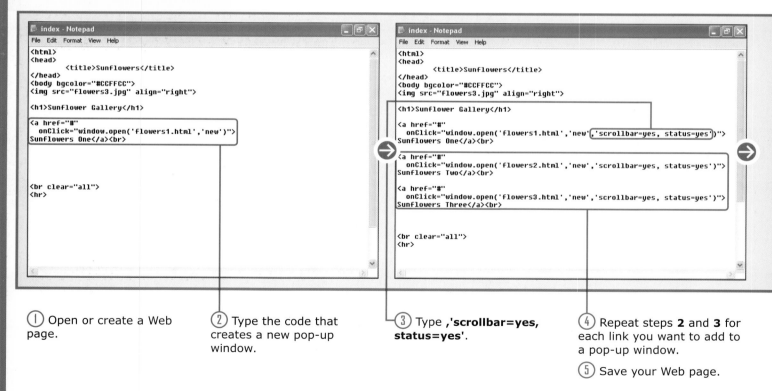

① Open or create a Web page.

② Type the code that creates a new pop-up window.

③ Type `,'scrollbar=yes, status=yes'`.

④ Repeat steps **2** and **3** for each link you want to add to a pop-up window.

⑤ Save your Web page.

Customize It! ☀

You can use a number of different properties to customize the appearance and function of a pop-up window that you create with the window.open statement.

Pop-Up Window Properties	
Property	*Purpose*
width	The width of the pop-up window.
height	The height of the pop-up window.
left	The distance from the left border to place the pop-up window.
top	The distance from the top border to place the pop-up window.
location	Whether the location bar displays.
menubar	Whether the menu bar displays.
toolbar	Whether the toolbar displays.
resizble	Whether a user can resize the window.
fullscreen	Whether the pop-up window should be maximized.

DIFFICULTY LEVEL

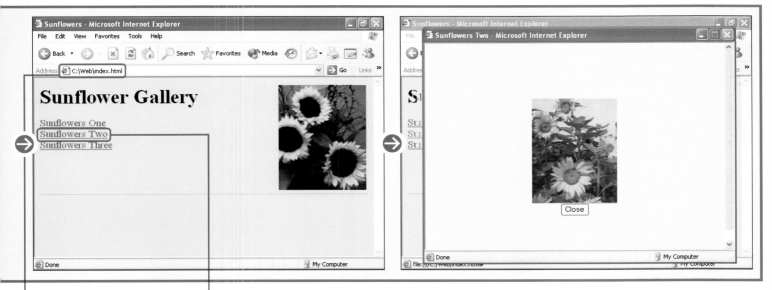

⑥ Type the location of the Web page in your Web browser address bar.

⑦ Press Enter.

⑧ Click the link to the pop-up window.

○ The pop-up window displays with a scrollbar and a status bar.

Display an
ALERT MESSAGE

You can display a message to users in a separate message box so that they can read any important information that you want them to view. You typically use message boxes only for very important messages. For example, you can make the message about an offer that is about to expire or an offer that only members can access on your Web site.

The alert statement generates a message box. Each message box contains a button that the user must click before the alert message disappears. The user

generally cannot to continue viewing your Web pages until they click the confirmation button in the message box.

You can specify the text that you want to appear in the message box. You should limit the size of text messages in a message box to no longer than a few sentences. The text message in the message box is the sole argument of the alert statement.

You can cause an alert message to display when a user clicks an image by using the onClick event with an img tag.

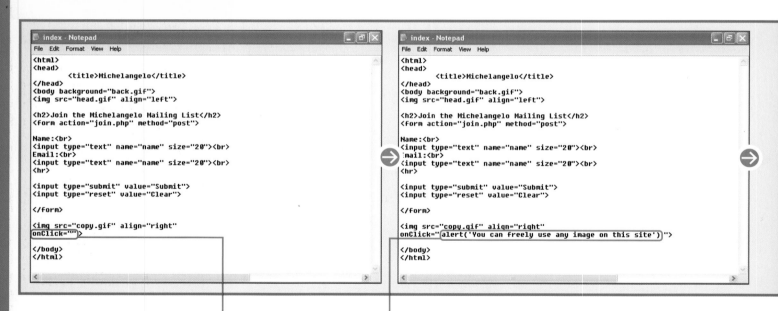

① Open or create a Web page that contains an image.

② Type **onClick=""** in the image tag.

③ Type **alert('?')**, replacing ? with the text you want to appear in the message box.

④ Save your Web page.

Caution! ☀

Message boxes interrupt users
when they are browsing your Web
site, because the users have to click
the button in the message box before
they can continue to view your Web pages.
For this reason, make sure that the information
you place in a message box is important. Using
too many message boxes on your Web site may
annoy your readers instead of helping them.

Did You Know? ☀

The appearance of the message boxes
depends on the type of Web browser in use
as well as the type of operating system that
is running the Web browser. Unlike pop-up
windows, message boxes offer you very little
control over their appearance.

DIFFICULTY LEVEL

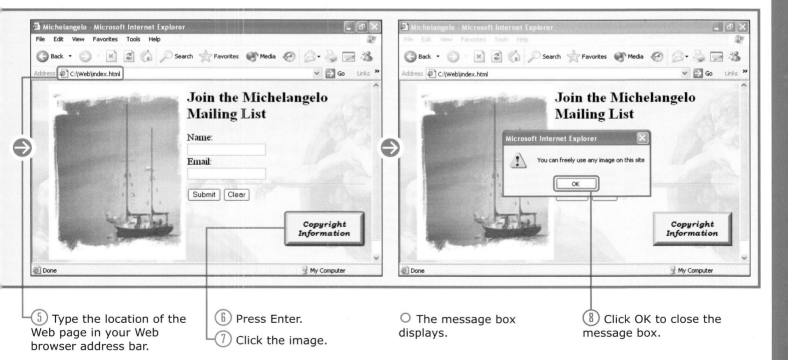

⑤ Type the location of the
Web page in your Web
browser address bar.

⑥ Press Enter.

⑦ Click the image.

○ The message box
displays.

⑧ Click OK to close the
message box.

Disable the RIGHT MOUSE BUTTON

You can disable the menu that appears when a user clicks the right mouse button. By disabling this menu, you make it harder for users to copy or print your Web pages.

The menu that appears when a user right-clicks a mouse allows the user to perform various functions, such as printing or copying items on a Web page.

Disabling the right mouse menu does not make it impossible for a user to copy or print your Web pages, but it does make it more difficult. There is no

function on the right mouse button menu that a user cannot access from other Web browser menus.

To disable the right button menu, you must create a function that determines if the user pressed the right mouse button. If so, a message box displays, and the return false statement ends the JavaScript processing.

You assign the function that checks whether the user clicks the right mouse button to the onmousedown property of the document object.

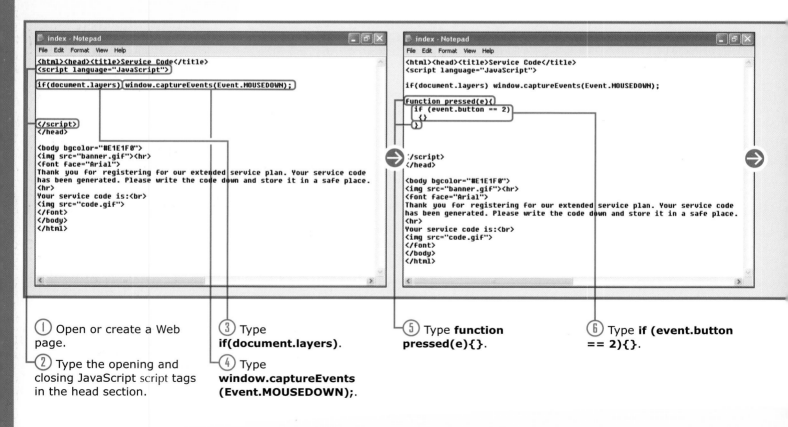

① Open or create a Web page.

② Type the opening and closing JavaScript script tags in the head section.

③ Type **if(document.layers)**.

④ Type **window.captureEvents (Event.MOUSEDOWN);**.

⑤ Type **function pressed(e){}**.

⑥ Type **if (event.button == 2){}**.

Caution!

Because it may annoy many users to find that you have disabled the right mouse menu, you should not disable it unless doing so provides a definite benefit. For example, you you disable the right mouse menu making it harder for a user to copy sensitive images.

Apply It!

Some mouse devices have more than two buttons, or can be configured to emulate a mouse with more than one button. To check whether a user is clicking other mouse buttons, you can use the or symbol || between multiple arguments of the if statement that checks whether a user is pressing mouse buttons.

```
if (event.button == 2 || event.button == 3) {
alert('Disabled');return false; }
```

82

DIFFICULTY LEVEL

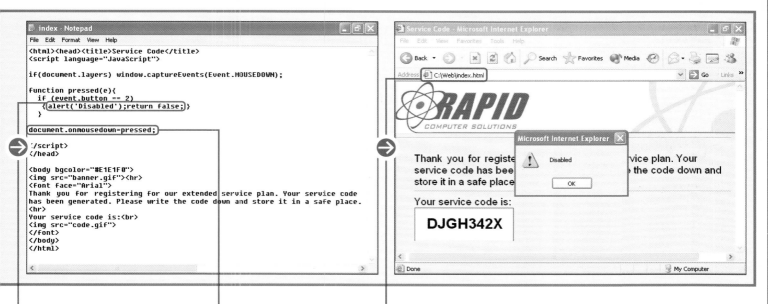

⑦ Type **alert('?');return false;**, replacing ? with the text you want to appear in the message box.

⑧ Type **document.onmouse down=pressed;**.

⑨ Save your Web page.

⑩ Type the location of the Web page in your Web browser address bar.

⑪ Press Enter.

⑫ Right-click the image.

○ The message box displays.

You can create a drop-down list that allows your users to access other Web pages in your Web site. A drop-down list that you use as a menu is called an *active drop-down menu*.

You can create a drop-down menu using a form with a drop-down list. You must make the value for each option tag the name of the Web page that you want to display in the Web browser when a user selects the option.

You can use an input tag with a type attribute set to a value of button to take users to the Web page they select. The JavaScript code reads the name of the Web page from the value of the option they select, and then changes the Web page that displays to the selected Web page. You must ensure that the opening form tag has a name attribute so that the JavaScript code can properly identify the form that contains the active drop-down menu.

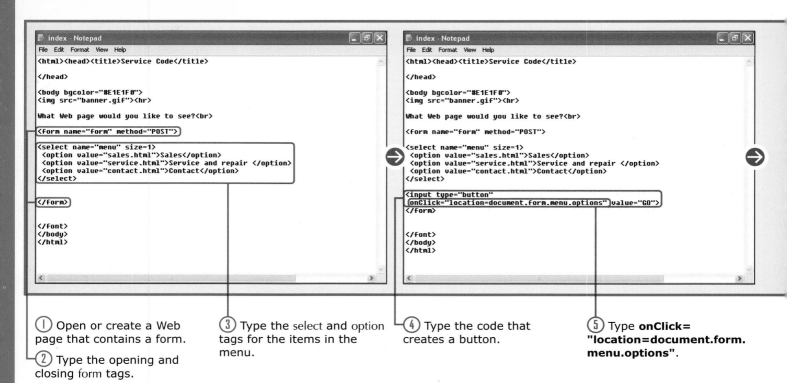

① Open or create a Web page that contains a form.

② Type the opening and closing form tags.

③ Type the select and option tags for the items in the menu.

④ Type the code that creates a button.

⑤ Type **onClick= "location=document.form. menu.options"**.

Caution! ☀

You must ensure that you enclose the code for the drop-down list within a separate set of form tags. Although you can have other forms on the same Web page as the active drop-down menu form, you cannot make the active drop-down list a part of another form.

DIFFICULTY LEVEL

Apply It! ☀

You do not have to link to just Web pages on your own Web site. You can also link to other pages on the Internet by specifying the URL of the Web page to link to, for example:

```
<option value="">Service</option>
```

Apply It! ☀

You can open a Web page you select in the drop-down menu in a new pop-up window by using the onClick event.

```
onClick="window.open( document.form.menu.options
[document. form.menu.selectedIndex].value, 'new'" );"
```

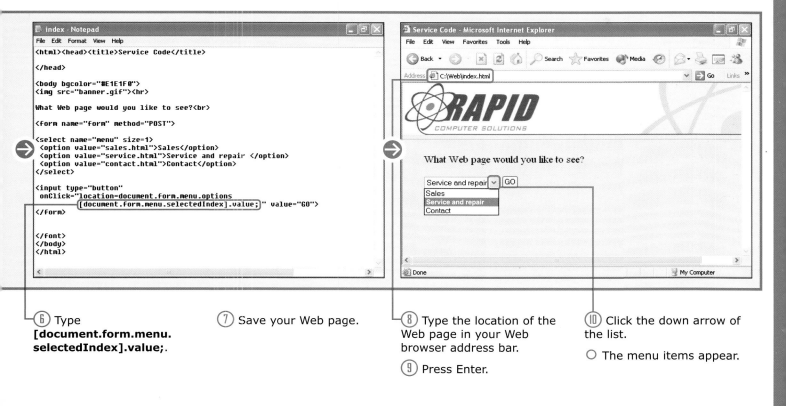

⑥ Type **[document.form.menu. selectedIndex].value;**.

⑦ Save your Web page.

⑧ Type the location of the Web page in your Web browser address bar.

⑨ Press Enter.

⑩ Click the down arrow of the list.

○ The menu items appear.

DYNAMICALLY CHANGING IMAGES

You can insert dynamically changing images into your Web page to make the Web page more interesting.

You can use the setInterval JavaScript statement for each image that you want to include in the collection of rotating images. The setInterval statement processes JavaScript code at time intervals that you can specify. You must enclose all the setInterval statements that you use within script tags in the head section of the HTML code.

The setInterval statement takes two arguments. The first argument contains the name that identifies the

image on the Web page and the name of the new image with which you want to replace it. The second argument of the setInterval statement is the amount of time, in milliseconds, you want the Web browser to wait before displaying the image.

You must place an image within the Web page and use the name attribute of the img tag to identify the image. The JavaScript code can then use this name to identify the image you want to replace. You should make all images the same size.

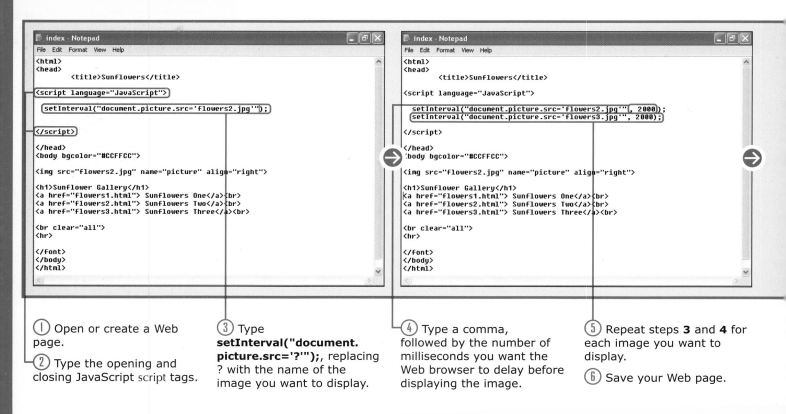

① Open or create a Web page.

② Type the opening and closing JavaScript script tags.

③ Type **setInterval("document. picture.src='?'");**, replacing ? with the name of the image you want to display.

④ Type a comma, followed by the number of milliseconds you want the Web browser to delay before displaying the image.

⑤ Repeat steps **3** and **4** for each image you want to display.

⑥ Save your Web page.

DIFFICULTY LEVEL

Apply It!

You can place an a tag
around a rotating image so that
it becomes a link.

```
<a href="gallery.html>
    <a img src="logo" name="picture">
</a>
```

Apply It!

You can specify the amount of time in the setInterval
statement in milliseconds, or thousandths of a second. For
example, for a time interval of five seconds, you specify a
wait time of 5000. You should always
specify a time interval that lets your user
view the entire image.

Caution!

Each image that you specify with the setInterval
statement must load in the Web browser before
it displays. Using large or numerous images slows
down the amount of time it takes for your Web
page to load and display.

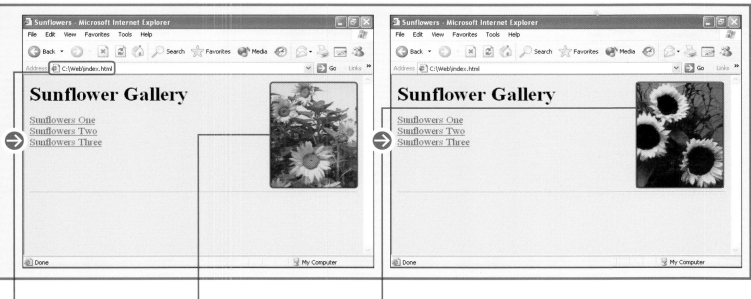

⑦ Type the location of the Web page in your Web browser address bar.

⑧ Press Enter.

○ After a delay, a new image appears.

○ After another delay, another new image appears.

Detect the WEB BROWSER INFORMATION

You can detect relevant information such as the type of Web browser with which a user accesses your Web page. You may find this useful if you want to display different information for users of different Web browsers or for users with browsers of differing capabilities.

There is a wide range of information about a Web browser that you can use the JavaScript code in your Web page to detect. JavaScript has properties that store information about the Web browser

accessing your Web page. You can assign the values of these properties to variables to make it easy to access those values later on.

You can use JavaScript to detect the name of a Web browser. Each Web browser also has a version number that you can detect. The Web browser name and version number are probably the most relevant information that you can detect about a Web browser.

You can also detect other less important items of information such as the code name of the Web browser and the user agent, which is the text that a Web browser uses to identify itself.

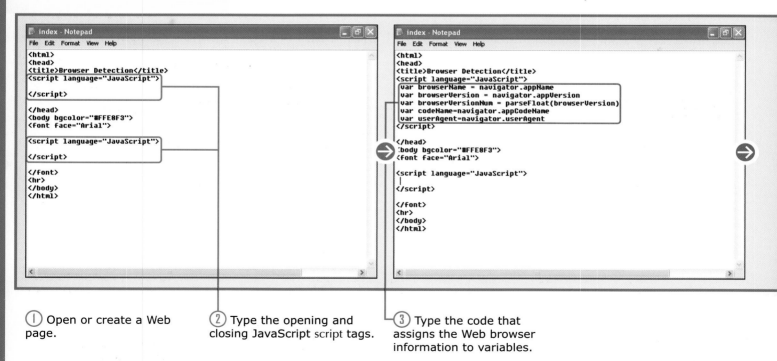

① Open or create a Web page.

② Type the opening and closing JavaScript script tags.

③ Type the code that assigns the Web browser information to variables.

Apply It!

The JavaScript if-else statement allows you to effectively use information about the different features of a Web browser accessing your Web page. For example:

```
If (browserName == "Microsoft Internet Explorer"){
document.write("<h2>You are using Internet Explorer</h2>"
    } else {
document.write("<h2>You are NOT using Internet Explorer</h2>"
    }
```

Caution!

Many Web browsers allow their users to override the identifying features of the Web browser, so that they can appear different from what the JavaScript code in your Web page detects.

Did You Know?

Not only do Web browsers have identifying information, but you can also detect information from other applications such as search engines that access your Web site.

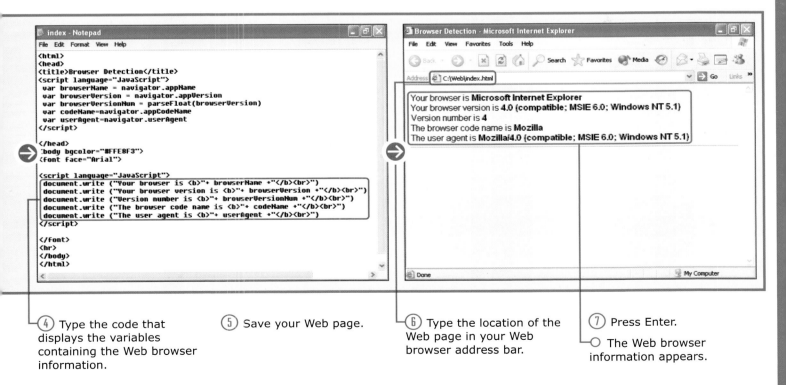

④ Type the code that displays the variables containing the Web browser information.

⑤ Save your Web page.

─⑥ Type the location of the Web page in your Web browser address bar.

⑦ Press Enter.

─O The Web browser information appears.

SCREEN RESOLUTION

You can detect the screen resolution of a computer that accesses your Web page. This may allow you to better lay out your Web page to match the size of the screen. You can specify screen resolution as the width of the display followed by the height of the display. Screen resolution is measured in pixels, and there are a number of common display resolutions in use. The three most common display resolutions are 640 x 480, 800 x 600, and 1024 x 768. The higher the resolution you have, the more detail and more items that a screen can display at one time.

You can store the display size in two JavaScript properties, screen.width and screen.height. The width and height properties only report the maximum resolution of the display; a user may resize a Web browser window to a smaller or bigger size than the total area of the display. Although a screen may have certain height and width values, this does not necessarily reflect the size of the Web browser window with which a user views your Web page.

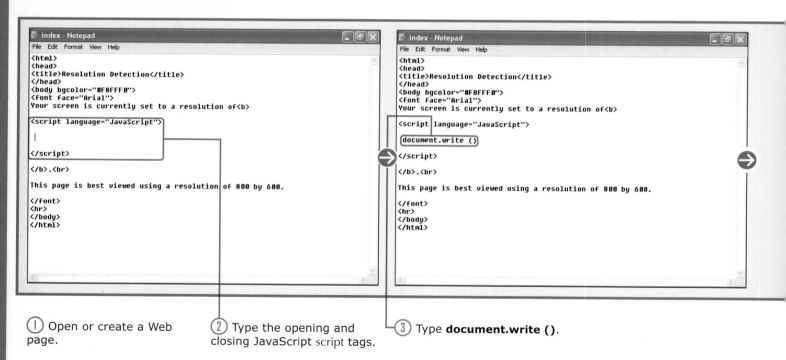

① Open or create a Web page.

② Type the opening and closing JavaScript script tags.

③ Type **document.write ()**.

Customize It!

You can specify the size and location of pop-up windows that your Web page opens. Using the width and height properties of the display, you can open a pop-up window position in the center of the display of a user. For example, to align a pop-up window that is 200 pixels wide with the center of the display, you must set the left-most position of the pop-up window to one-half of the display width minus 100.

Apply It!

As with all JavaScript properties, you may find the width and height properties most helpful when using them with an if statement. For example, you can display a message if you detect a low screen resolution:

```
if (screen.width < 800){
alert("Please increase your resolution)}
```

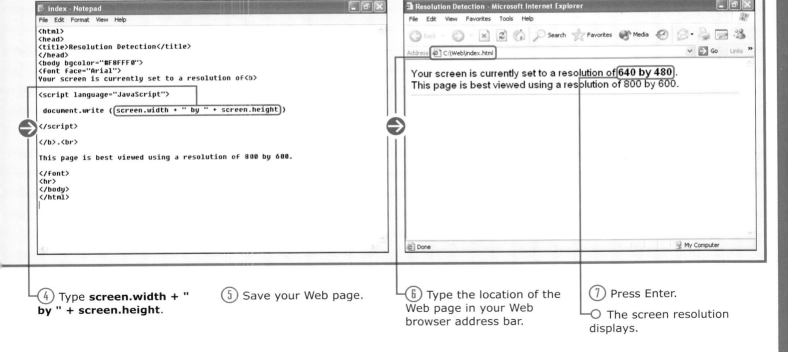

④ Type **screen.width + " by " + screen.height**.

⑤ Save your Web page.

⑥ Type the location of the Web page in your Web browser address bar.

⑦ Press Enter.

○ The screen resolution displays.

Using e-mail to
SHARE WEB PAGES

With JavaScript, you can make it easier for users to share your Web pages by sending an e-mail to share the location of your Web page. Sending a link increases the number of people who view your Web page. When the user selects the link, the e-mail program opens, and the user can simply enter the name of the recipient and then send the message. The information about your Web page remains in the message.

To send an e-mail, you create a large string of text with the e-mail information such as the subject and the body of the message. To include the link to your

Web page in the body of the message, you include the JavaScript property location.href in the body text. To make the text containing the e-mail information more manageable, you can assign the text to a variable and then set the location.href property to the value of the variable.

You can place the JavaScript code that creates the message in a function in the head section of the Web page, and then when a user clicks the link, the function processes.

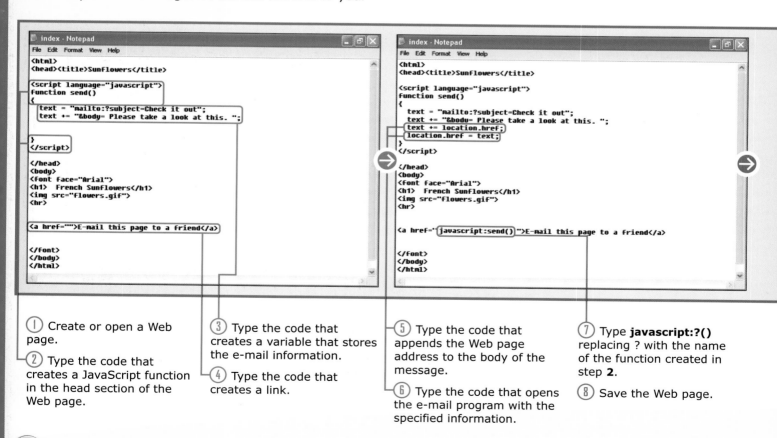

① Create or open a Web page.

② Type the code that creates a JavaScript function in the head section of the Web page.

③ Type the code that creates a variable that stores the e-mail information.

④ Type the code that creates a link.

⑤ Type the code that appends the Web page address to the body of the message.

⑥ Type the code that opens the e-mail program with the specified information.

⑦ Type **javascript:?()** replacing ? with the name of the function created in step **2**.

⑧ Save the Web page.

DIFFICULTY LEVEL

Caution!
Whenever you use a link to allow users to send links to your page, you should make the text of the link as descriptive as possible. This prevents users from inadvertently thinking the link is to another Web page.

Apply It!
E-mail links are great on Web pages that users want to share with others. Schedules, special offers, or news items are good examples of Web pages that users find useful to share.

Apply It!
Using the onMouseUp attribute of the img tag, you can easily use an image instead of a link to allow users to share your Web pages.

< img src="email.gif" onMouseUp="javascript:send()">.

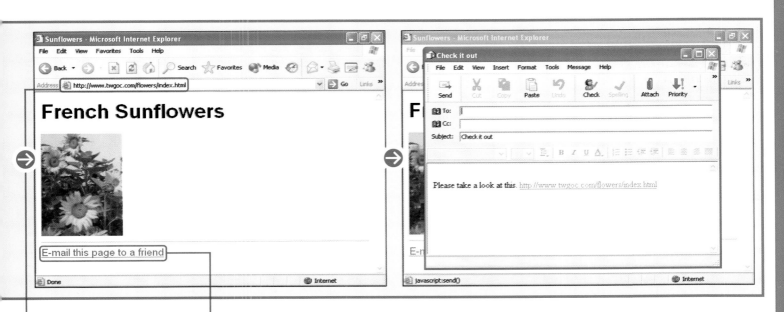

⑨ Type the location of the Web page in your Web browser address bar.

⑩ Press Enter.

⑪ Click the link that allows you to share the Web page.

○ The e-mail program starts with the Web page information in the body of the message.

You can increase or decrease the size of an item on your Web page to allow users to enlarge or reduce its size. You can change the size of images to allow users to examine the image or you can increase the size of text to make your Web pages easier to read for users who are visually impaired.

To identify an item whose size you want to allow a user to change, you can use the id attribute to specify a name for the tag. You must make the id value unique for each item on the Web page.

You can create a button that allows the user to change the item size. The onMouseUp event lets you specify the JavaScript code that will process when a user clicks on the button. You can then use the JavaScript code to change the size of an item.

You use the style.zoom property of an item to set the magnification level of the item. At 100% the size is normal, while at 200% the size of the item will double.

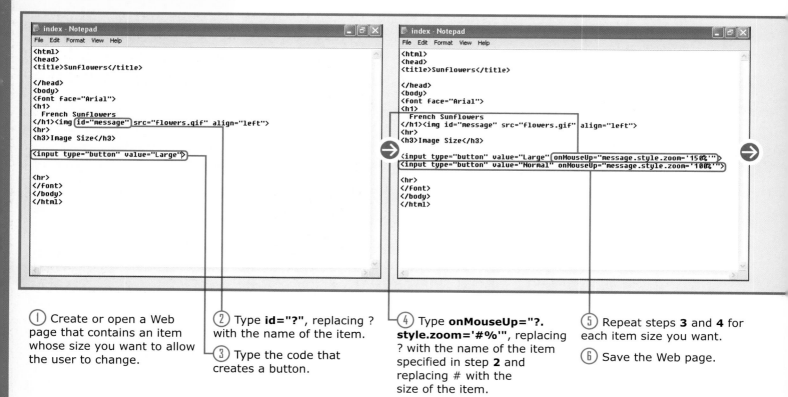

① Create or open a Web page that contains an item whose size you want to allow the user to change.

② Type **id="?"**, replacing ? with the name of the item.

③ Type the code that creates a button.

④ Type **onMouseUp="?. style.zoom='#%'"**, replacing ? with the name of the item specified in step **2** and replacing # with the size of the item.

⑤ Repeat steps **3** and **4** for each item size you want.

⑥ Save the Web page.

Caution! ※

When a user resizes items on
a Web page, the other items on
the page rearrange to accommodate
the newly sized item. This may adversely
affect the original layout of the Web page.
Whenever you allow the user to change the
size of items, you should make it easy for the
user to return the item to its original size.

Apply It! ※

You can also change the size of other items such
as text by using the id attribute of the tag
enclosing the text. For example, to allow users to
increase the size of a text header, simply use the id
tag to identify the text:

<h2 id="message">Welcome to the main games site</h2>

DIFFICULTY LEVEL

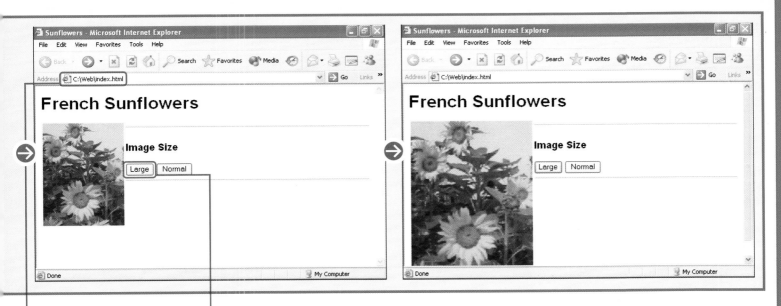

⑦ Type the location of the
Web page in your Web
browser address bar.

⑧ Press Enter.

⑨ Click the button that
changes the size of the item.

○ The item changes size.

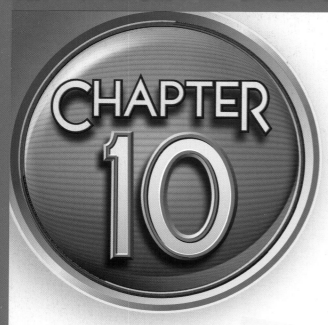

CHAPTER 10

Using Style Sheets to Enhance HTML

You can use style sheets to enhance the layout and appearance capabilities of HTML. Using style sheets enables you to exert far more control over the objects on a Web page than is possible with just HTML code. For example, you can use style sheets to place images at precise coordinates on a Web page.

You can incorporate style sheets into your HTML code in a number of ways. When creating an item on a Web page, you can add style sheet information to the tag that creates that item. For example, when using styles to align an image on the Web page, you can place the style information in the img tag that creates the image. You can apply any style information that you want

to add to the HTML tag using a style attribute and you can add style attributes to almost any HTML tag.

You can place more extensive style information in the head section of the HTML code. Items in the Web page can then access that information when they require it. It is also possible to place style information in a separate file that you store with the HTML code that uses the style information.

You can specify the style information itself using a series of properties and property values. You can use the same property for different items; for example, you can use the background-color property to set the background color of the Web page or of a paragraph of text.

TOP 100

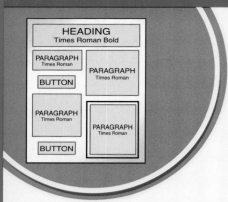

Add style by changing the
SCROLLBAR COLORS

You can change the color of a Web browser scroll bar to match the color scheme of your Web page. A scroll bar contains arrows that allow a user to move through the Web page when the page is larger than the Web browser window.

A slider also appears on the track section of the scroll bar. A user can click and drag the slider across the track to scroll through the contents of the Web page.

You can change the color of the scroll bar with a style block in the head section of the Web page. You can specify values for style sheet properties that control how the scroll bar appears.

The scrollbar-face-color property determines the color of the up and down arrows area and the slider. The scrollbar-arrow-color property governs the color of the arrows themselves. You can control the color of the track on which the slider moves with the scrollbar-track-color property.

The color of the scroll bar reverts to normal when you view a Web page that contains no style information dictating the scroll bar color.

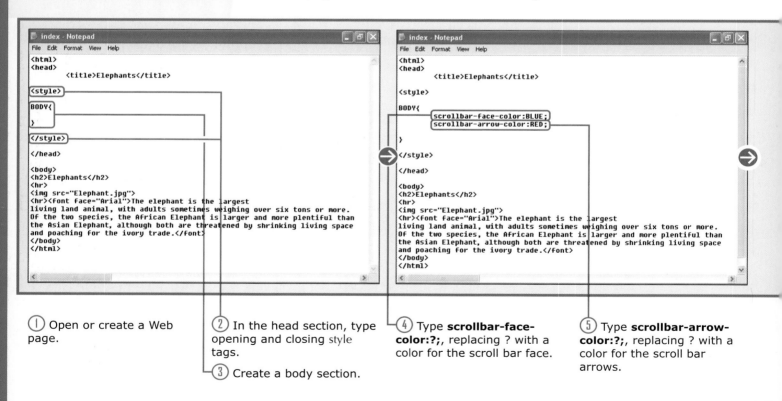

① Open or create a Web page.

② In the head section, type opening and closing style tags.

③ Create a body section.

④ Type **scrollbar-face-color:?;**, replacing ? with a color for the scroll bar face.

⑤ Type **scrollbar-arrow-color:?;**, replacing ? with a color for the scroll bar arrows.

Did You Know? ※

Scroll bars appear automatically whenever a Web page does not completely fit into a Web browser window. If your Web page fits inside a Web browser window, even if you have specified colors for the scroll bar, the scroll bars may not appear.

DIFFICULTY LEVEL

Customize It! ※

You can use other style properties to control the appearance of the scroll bar.

Additional Scroll Bar Style Properties	
Property	*Description*
scrollbar-shadow-color	The bottom and right edges of the slider and arrow boxes.
scrollbar-highlight-color	The top and left edges of the slider and arrow boxes.
scrollbar-darkshadow-color	The sides of the scroll bar.

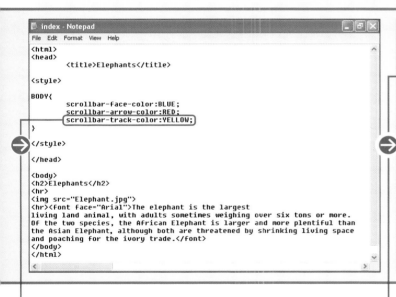

⑥ Type **scrollbar-track-color:?;**, replacing ? with a color for the scroll bar track.

⑦ Save your Web page.

⑧ Type the location of the Web page in your Web browser address bar.

⑨ Press Enter.

○ The Web page displays with the colored scroll bar.

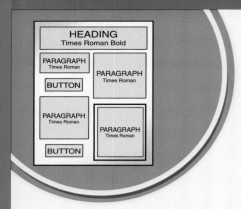

Change the
MOUSE POINTER
STYLE

You can change the appearance of the mouse pointer as it moves over items on your Web page. This feature gives the user more information about the items on your Web page. For example, if your Web page contains a link to another Web page with more information about an item, you can cause the mouse pointer to change to a question mark when it moves over the link.

You can add a style attribute to the tag of any item for which you want the pointer to change when it moves over the item. The style attribute contains the

cursor property, and a value that indicates the pointer type you desire. For example, the value pointer changes the mouse pointer from an arrowhead to a hand with a pointing finger.

The pointer that replaces the default pointer depends on the operating system of the computer that accesses your Web page, and what types of cursors the user selects. Most operating systems allow users to customize the appearance of the mouse pointers.

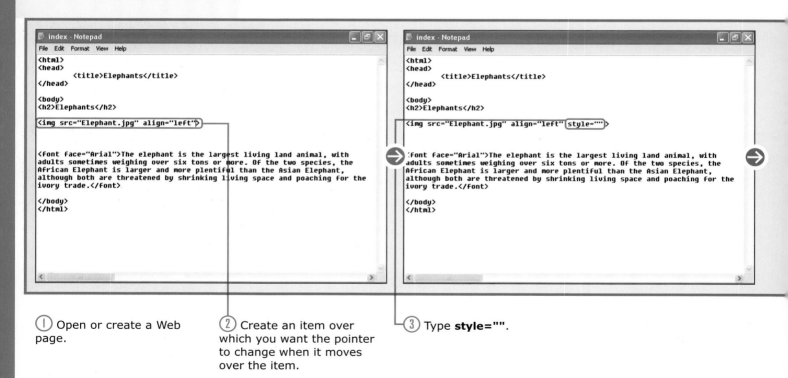

① Open or create a Web page.

② Create an item over which you want the pointer to change when it moves over the item.

③ Type **style=""**.

Apply It! ※

You can change the pointer whenever it moves over any elements on the Web page by applying the style to the body tag of the Web page.

`<body style="cursor: pointer;">`

Customize It! ※

There are many values for the cursor property that you can use to change the appearance of the mouse pointer.

Pointer Types	
Value	*Typical Appearance*
crosshair	A plus symbol
default	The original mouse pointer
pointer	A hand with a pointing finger
move	A crosshair with arrowheads
text	A single upright line
wait	An hourglass
help	An arrowhead with a question mark

DIFFICULTY LEVEL

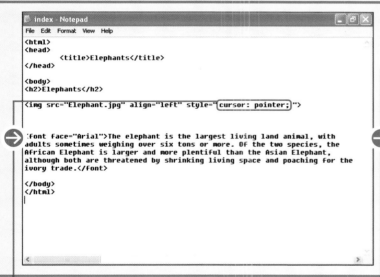

④ Type **cursor:?;**, replacing ? with the kind of pointer to which you want the mouse pointer to change.

⑤ Save your Web page.

⑥ Type the location of the Web page in your Web browser address bar.

⑦ Press Enter.

⑧ Move the mouse pointer over the item.

○ The mouse pointer changes from an arrow to a different pointer.

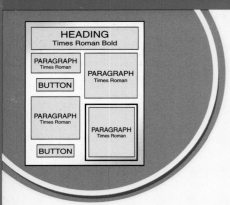

Using style sheets to PRECISELY ALIGN ITEMS

You can use style sheets to precisely align items on a Web page. Style sheets allow you to specify the precise location of items such as images and text on a Web page. You can specify how far from the side of the Web browser window you want to place an item. Placing an item in relation to the side of the Web browser window is referred to as positioning the item *absolutely*.

You can use the position property with the absolute value to place items absolutely. Once you specify the position property, you can use a second property,

either top, bottom, left, or right, to specify the side of the Web browser window with which you want to align items. The value of this property is the distance from the side of the window in pixels.

The exact positions of the items change, depending on the size of the Web browser window. In turn, the window size changes, depending on the resolution and size of the display, and whether the user resizes the Web browser window.

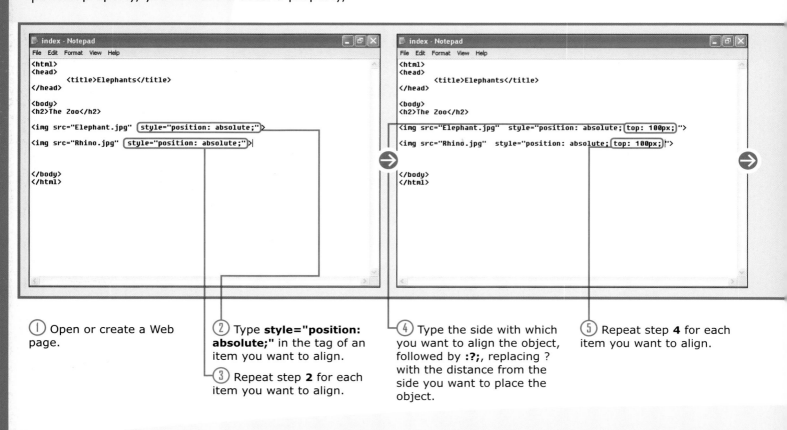

① Open or create a Web page.

② Type **style="position: absolute;"** in the tag of an item you want to align.

③ Repeat step **2** for each item you want to align.

④ Type the side with which you want to align the object, followed by **:?;**, replacing ? with the distance from the side you want to place the object.

⑤ Repeat step **4** for each item you want to align.

Apply It! ☀

The use of the absolute value
of the position property places
items in relation to the side of the
Web browser window. To position items
relative from the items' intended place on
the Web page, use the relative value:

{position: relative;}

Customize It! ☀

Apart from pixels, you can also specify distance
by replacing the letters px with another notation.

Distance Specifications	
Notation	*Distance*
mm	Millimeters
cm	Centimeters
in	Inches
pt	Points
pc	Picas

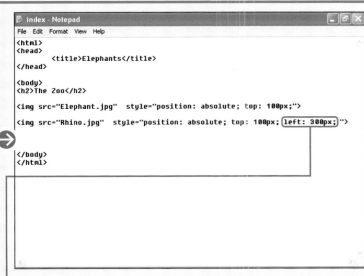

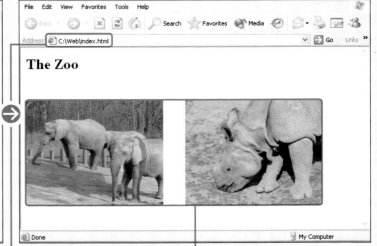

⑥ Type the side with which
you want to align the object,
followed by **:?;**, replacing ?
with the distance from the
side you want to place the
object.

⑦ Save your Web page.

⑧ Type the location of the
Web page in your Web
browser address bar.

⑨ Press Enter.

○ The Web page displays
with the items aligned.

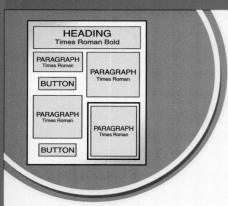

Boost a Web page with
COLORED BUTTONS

You can create buttons on a Web page to provide a user with a more informative and attractive way of accessing a link to another Web page. You can also change the color of buttons using styles.

You can create buttons with the button tag. To convert a button to a link, you can use the onClick attribute to access a section of JavaScript code that loads a new Web page when the user clicks the button. Any text within the opening and closing button tag appears on the button.

Within the style attribute of the button tag, you can use the background-color property to set the color of the button. You can make the color of the button any valid HTML color code.

You can also use styles to specify the size of the font that appears on the button. You can specify a point size for the font by appending pt to the numerical value of the font size.

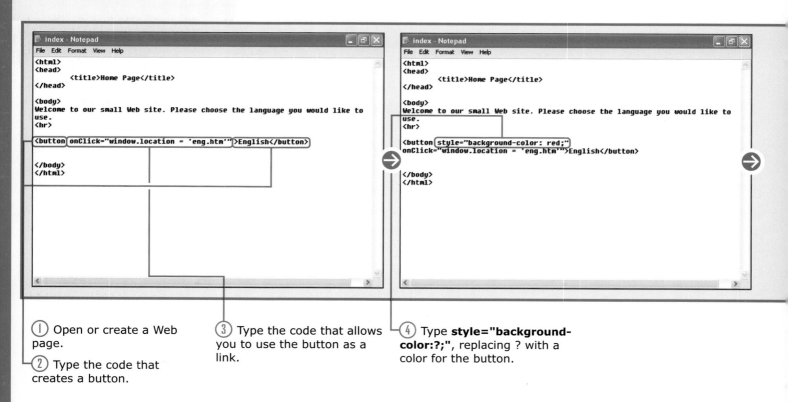

① Open or create a Web page.

② Type the code that creates a button.

③ Type the code that allows you to use the button as a link.

④ Type **style="background-color:?;"**, replacing ? with a color for the button.

92

DIFFICULTY LEVEL

Apply It! ※

You can use the style attribute
of the button tag to apply styles to
individual buttons. You can apply the
same formatting to all buttons in the
Web page by using a style block in the head
section of the Web page. For example:

```
<style type="text/css">
button{background-color: red; font-size: 14pt;}
</style>
```

Did You Know? ※

When you apply HTML color codes, you
can specify one of the more well-known
colors such as red or white, or you can use a
color code preceded by a hash symbol, #, as
in #00FFFF for the color aqua, or #00FF00 for
the color lime.

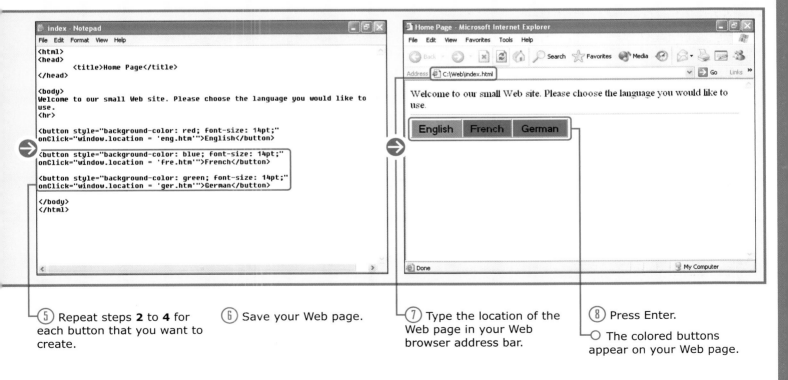

⑤ Repeat steps **2** to **4** for each button that you want to create.

⑥ Save your Web page.

⑦ Type the location of the Web page in your Web browser address bar.

⑧ Press Enter.

○ The colored buttons appear on your Web page.

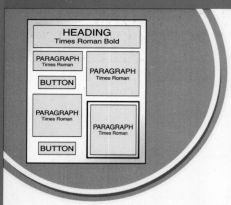

Quickly
CHANGE THE LOOK
of all Web pages

You can use style sheets to enhance the capabilities of HTML code in a Web page, and to change the appearance of the Web page. You can create style information in a single, external file that other Web pages can access. When you change the information in that file, the changes instantly appear in all the Web pages that use that style sheet.

You can create the external style sheet with a text editor. In the style sheet, you can define the properties of the tags you want to change. You should save the style sheet file with the .css file extension.

Once you save the style sheet file, you can instruct Web pages to retrieve information from the style sheet file using the link tag. You must place the link tag in the head section of the Web page. The link tag contains the rel attribute with a value of stylesheet, which indicates that the Web page links to a style sheet file. The href attribute specifies the name of the style sheet file.

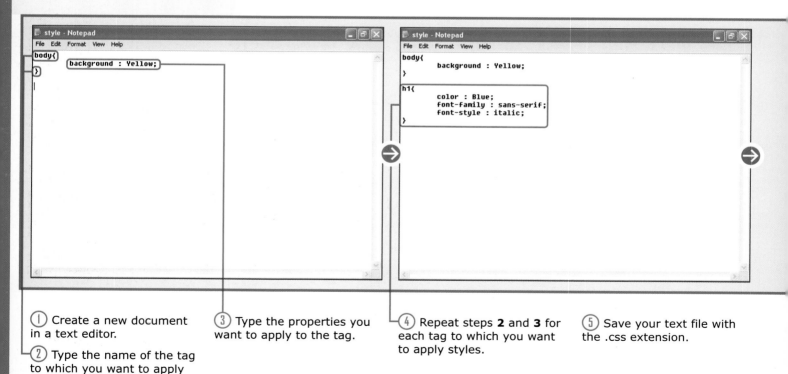

① Create a new document in a text editor.

② Type the name of the tag to which you want to apply styles, followed by **{}**.

③ Type the properties you want to apply to the tag.

④ Repeat steps **2** and **3** for each tag to which you want to apply styles.

⑤ Save your text file with the .css extension.

Did You Know? ※

You can apply many style sheet properties to HTML elements. For more complete information about style sheets and their available properties, refer to the style sheet section of the World Wide Web Consortium Web site at: http://www.w3.org/Style/CSS/

Apply It! ※

Style sheet files can become large and complicated, making them hard to read. You can add comments to the style sheet file by placing the comments between /* and */, for example:

/* Web site style sheet number 2 */

Apply It! ※

You can define the same properties for multiple HTML tags in a style sheet by separating each tag name with a comma, for example:

p, h1, h2 { font-style : italic;}

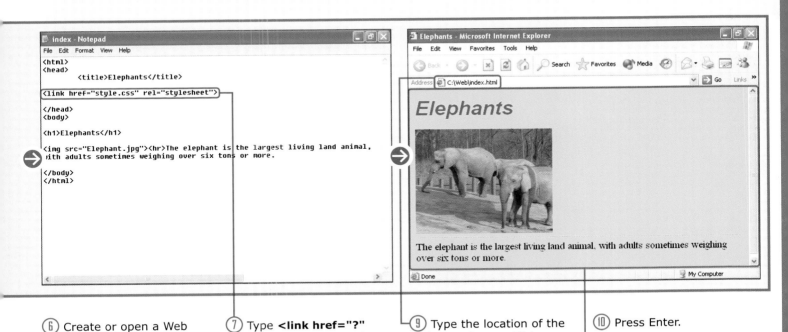

⑥ Create or open a Web page.

⑦ Type **<link href="?" rel="stylesheet">**, replacing ? with the name of the file you specified in step **5**.

⑧ Save your Web page.

⑨ Type the location of the Web page in your Web browser address bar.

⑩ Press Enter.

○ The Web page displays with the styles applied.

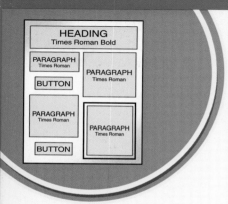

You can use style sheets to add borders to items on your Web page. Normally, when you use HTML, you must have tables to create the appearance of borders around items. With styles, you can create borders for many different types of HTML elements, including text and headers.

Along with solid borders, styles let you choose from different border patterns, such as dots or dashes. These choices give you more flexibility in designing the look of your Web page.

You can specify the characteristics of a border using the border-style property. The values of the property typically include the border style, such as dashed or dotted, as well as the color of the border. You can use any valid HTML value for the border color. You can also specify the thickness of the border as either thin, medium, or thick.

Many older Web browsers do not support the use of any type of style information and may not recognize display borders that you specify with styles.

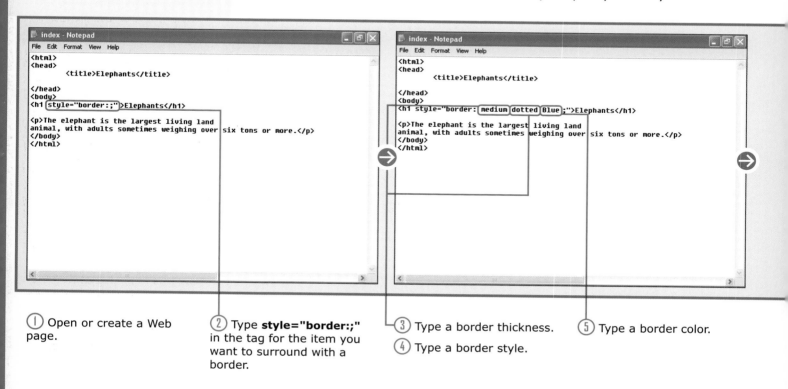

① Open or create a Web page.

② Type **style="border:;"** in the tag for the item you want to surround with a border.

③ Type a border thickness.

④ Type a border style.

⑤ Type a border color.

Apply It!

You can also specify the exact
thickness of a border in pixels.
When specifying the border style,
simply include how wide you want the
border to be, followed by px. For example:

style="border: 10px dotted Blue;"

Apply It!

The different sides of a border can have their own
individual colors if you specify the
border color using the border-color
property. You can specify the colors for
each side in this order: top, right side,
bottom, left side, for example:

border-color: Blue Fuchsia Green Red;

DIFFICULTY LEVEL

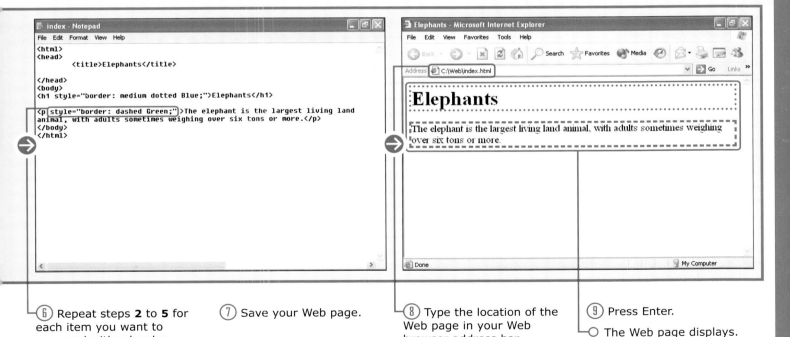

⑥ Repeat steps **2** to **5** for each item you want to surround with a border.

⑦ Save your Web page.

⑧ Type the location of the Web page in your Web browser address bar.

⑨ Press Enter.
○ The Web page displays.

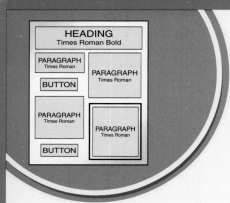

Place
TEXT IN COLUMNS

You can use style sheets to format text into columns of text, similar to a newspaper format. To give a Web page the appearance of a newspaper, the text in the columns must align with both sides of the column. This type of alignment is called *justifying the text*. Justifying the text allows the Web browser to automatically adjust the spacing between words so that the text aligns on both sides.

To stop adjacent columns of text from appearing as one, you can specify a margin distance to set the margins around each column of text.

You can use the float property with a value of left to allow the columns of data to appear side-by-side. You can specify the width of the column as a percentage of the width of the Web browser window. There is no limit to how many columns of text you can have in a Web page, although a maximum of three or four ensures that your text remains readable.

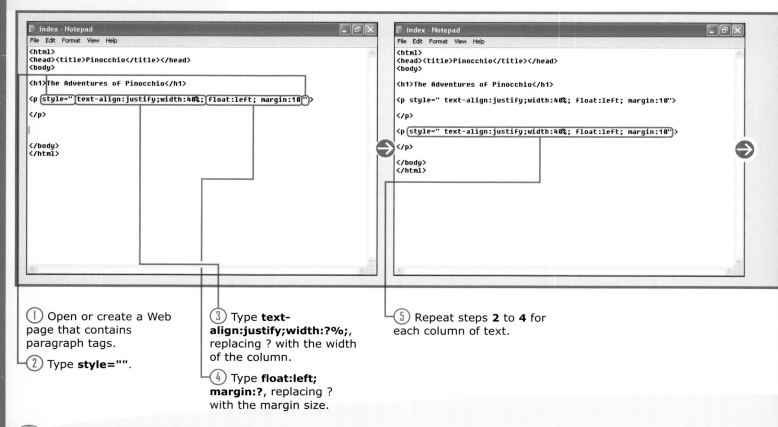

① Open or create a Web page that contains paragraph tags.

② Type **style=""**.

③ Type **text-align:justify;width:?%;**, replacing ? with the width of the column.

④ Type **float:left; margin:?**, replacing ? with the margin size.

⑤ Repeat steps **2** to **4** for each column of text.

Apply It! ※

You can use the same style information that formats columnar text with all text on a Web page that you enclose in a paragraph tag p. By specifying the style in a style block in the head section of your Web page, you avoid having to use the style attribute repeatedly within the p tag in your HTML code.

Caution! ※

Try not to create long columns of text on a Web page. Users may find it frustrating if they have to scroll up and down a Web page in order to read the content. If you do use columns of text, try to fit all the information onto a single screen.

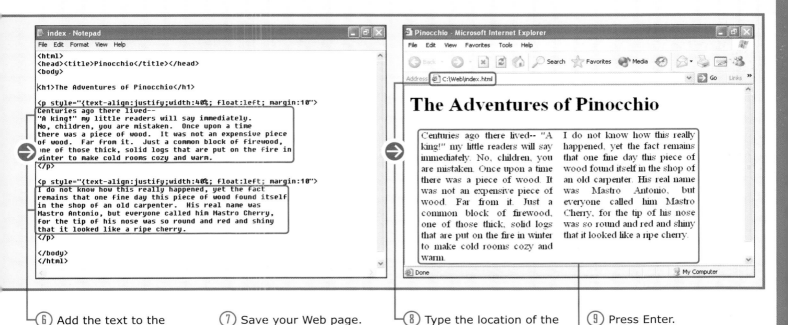

⑥ Add the text to the paragraph elements.

⑦ Save your Web page.

⑧ Type the location of the Web page in your Web browser address bar.

⑨ Press Enter.

○ The text displays in justified columns.

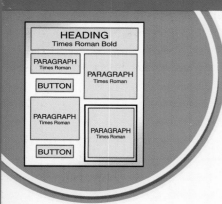

CREATE A SHADOW
behind text

You can use styles to create the effect of a shadow behind your text. A shadow can help draw attention to important information on your Web page, such as headers, or simply improve the appearance of the Web page.

You can create a shadow, or drop shadow, by placing a copy of your text underneath the original text, and then changing the color of the copied text. If you move the copied text down and to the right, it appears as a shadow.

To position text, such as a header, you can use a style attribute to specify the exact position of the text on your Web page. You can use the top and left properties to specify the position of the text. To use exact positioning, you must give the position property a value of absolute.

You can use the color property to set the color of the shadow text. When placing the text in your Web page, you should place the shadow text first, with the subsequent text over it.

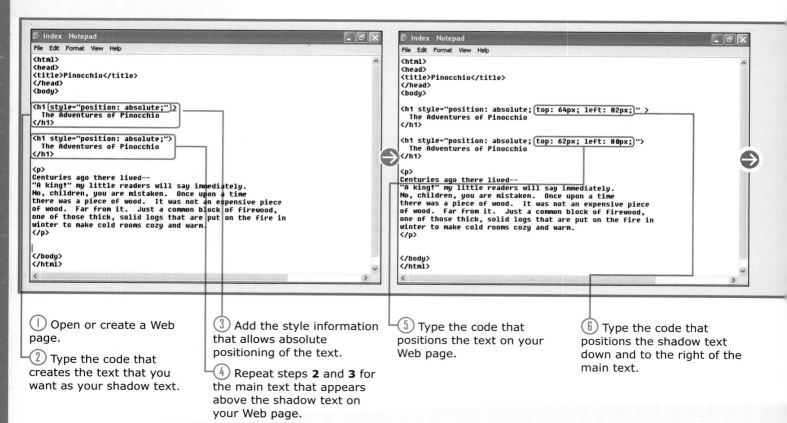

① Open or create a Web page.

② Type the code that creates the text that you want as your shadow text.

③ Add the style information that allows absolute positioning of the text.

④ Repeat steps **2** and **3** for the main text that appears above the shadow text on your Web page.

⑤ Type the code that positions the text on your Web page.

⑥ Type the code that positions the shadow text down and to the right of the main text.

Caution! ※

When you position items on a Web page using the position property with the absolute value, you should implicitly position the other items on the Web page. Otherwise, the other items on the Web page may display in a way that conflicts with the items that you have positioned using style sheets.

Did You Know? ※

Most image-editing programs enable you to quickly create drop shadows for text as well as any other elements on your Web page.

DIFFICULTY LEVEL

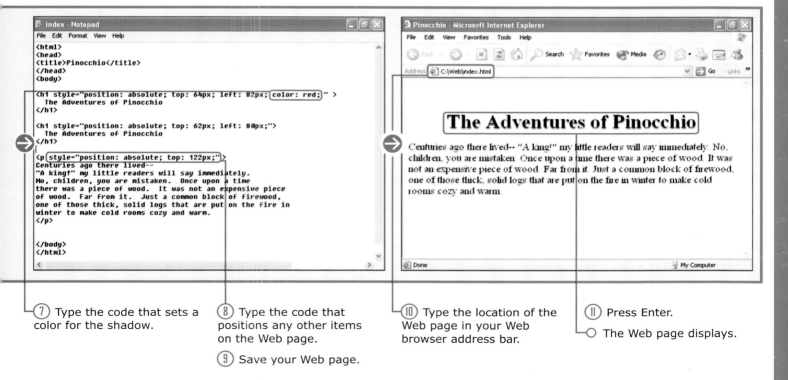

⑦ Type the code that sets a color for the shadow.

⑧ Type the code that positions any other items on the Web page.

⑨ Save your Web page.

⑩ Type the location of the Web page in your Web browser address bar.

⑪ Press Enter.

○ The Web page displays.

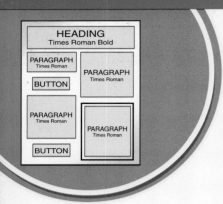

Create effects by
OVERLAPPING
TEXT AND IMAGES

You can overlap text and images to create interesting visual effects on your Web page. HTML code is designed to create elements on a Web page that flow around each other. You can use styles to prevent elements on a Web page from flowing around each other and to appear exactly where you want them on the Web page. If the positions of two elements conflict with one another, the latest object you create on the Web page appears above any other object that occupies the same space.

You can use styles to specify which objects you want to overlap by assigning each object a level. For example, an object with a level of 1 overlaps an object with a level of 0 or less. You do not have to use negative numbers to indicate a lower level; the code uses the relationship to the other level number and not the number itself. You can specify levels using the z-index property, and there is no limit to the number of levels you can have.

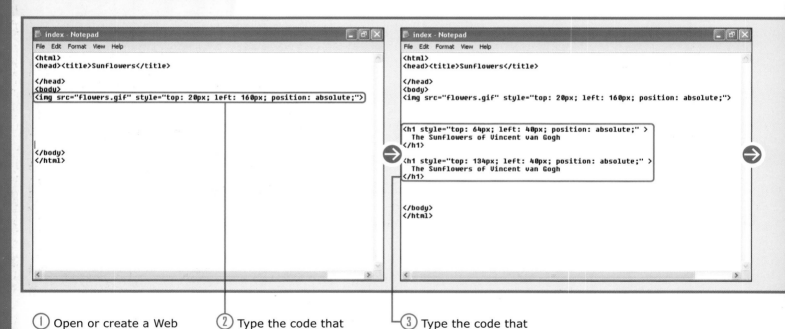

① Open or create a Web page.

② Type the code that absolutely positions an image on the Web page.

③ Type the code that positions other items that overlap the image you placed in step **2**.

DIFFICULTY LEVEL

Caution! ☀

Internet Explorer supports the z-index property. However, many older browsers, particularly from Netscape, do not support the z-index property.

Apply It! ☀

You can use the z-index property with many types of objects, not just text and images. For example, you can use the z-index property to assign levels to objects such as tables, inline frames, and buttons.

Did You Know? ☀

By default, the Web browser assigns a z-level value of 0 to any element that does not have a z-value property in its style attribute.

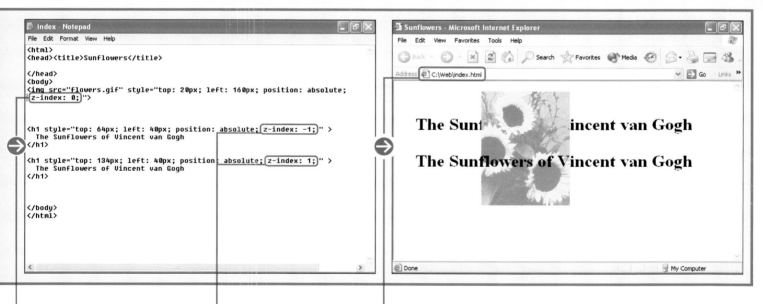

④ Type **z-index:?;**, replacing ? with a level number for the object.

⑤ Repeat step **4** for the other items on the Web page, using different level numbers.

⑥ Save your Web page.

⑦ Type the location of the Web page in your Web browser address bar.

⑧ Press Enter.

○ The overlapping items display.

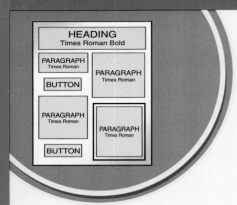

HIDE ITEMS
on a Web page

You can make objects on a Web page, such as images and text, invisible. You may want to make items invisible to help you lay out a page or to add items to a Web page that you want to appear later.

You can use the visibility property to either hide an item or make it visible. By default, all items on a Web page are visible, although you can state implicitly in the style attribute that an item is visible by setting the visibility property to visible.

Regardless of the item you want to make invisible, it still consumes space on the Web page. Other items

on the Web page are offset as if the item were visible. For example, if you place an invisible image on a Web page, the text may wrap around the image even though you do not see it.

The ability to hide items becomes very useful when you use it with a scripting language such as JavaScript, which allows you to hide items dynamically. For more information about JavaScript, see chapter 9.

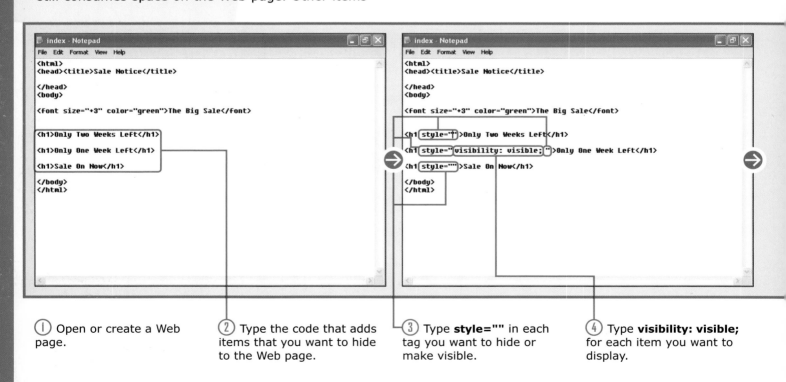

① Open or create a Web page.

② Type the code that adds items that you want to hide to the Web page.

③ Type **style=""** in each tag you want to hide or make visible.

④ Type **visibility: visible;** for each item you want to display.

Caution! ※

As with many features of style sheets, the visibility feature may not work with older Web browsers. This is not a concern if you are creating a Web page for an intranet or company Web site, or in instances where you know what Web browser your audience uses. However, if you are designing a Web site for the Internet and you use style sheets, there is a strong possibility that some of your users may not be able to view your Web pages as you intend.

Apply It! ※

You can apply the visibility property to many items, not just text and images. You can also hide tables, inline frames, links, and form elements.

DIFFICULTY LEVEL

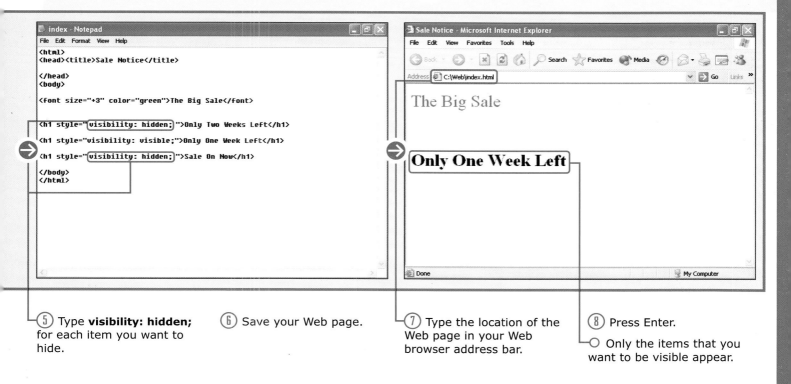

⑤ Type **visibility: hidden;** for each item you want to hide.

⑥ Save your Web page.

⑦ Type the location of the Web page in your Web browser address bar.

⑧ Press Enter.

○ Only the items that you want to be visible appear.

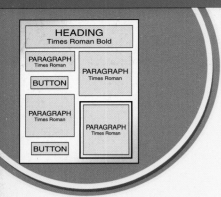

Position an
IMAGE IN THE
BACKGROUND

You can position background images to better control the layout of the images on your Web page. You control background images using the body tag. To apply style information about the background image to the body tag, you must create a body style block in the style section of the Web page.

The background-image: property specifies the name of the image that you want to use as the background image. The value of the background-image: property is url followed by a set of parentheses enclosing the file name.

You specify a single image that does not tile in the background using the background-repeat: property with the no-repeat value. If you do not specify the no-repeat value, the image tiles to fill the complete background.

To have the image stationary in the background instead of having it move when the Web page scrolls through, you specify the background-attachment: property with the value of fixed.

You indicate the actual position of the background image with the background-position: property. You can use values such as top, bottom, left and right to position the background image on the Web page.

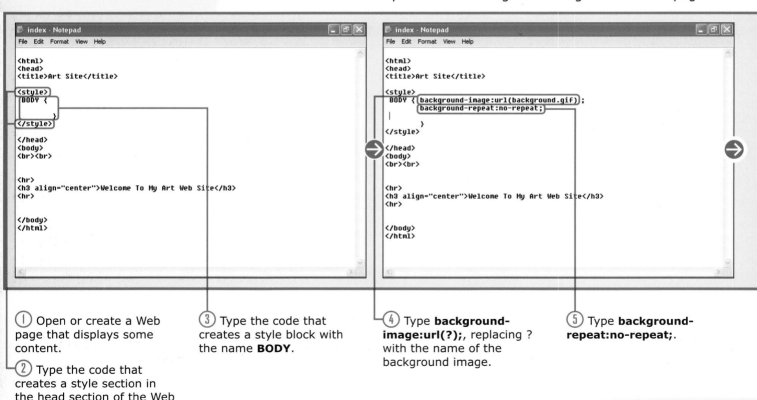

① Open or create a Web page that displays some content.

② Type the code that creates a style section in the head section of the Web page.

③ Type the code that creates a style block with the name **BODY**.

④ Type **background-image:url(?);**, replacing ? with the name of the background image.

⑤ Type **background-repeat:no-repeat;**.

DIFFICULTY LEVEL

Apply It! ※

You can also use the
background-image: property to
place a background image that is
located on another computer on the
network or the Internet. To use a
background image located on another
computer, you type the location of the
image on the network or Internet when
specifying the file name of the background
image:

background-image:url(http://www.rapidcomputer.com/images/logo.gif)

Apply It! ※

You can use a number of different types of
values to better position the background image.
The two values of the background-position specify the
left and then the right positioning. For example, to
place the background image halfway across the Web
page, 10 pixels from the top of the window, use:

background-position: 50%,10px;

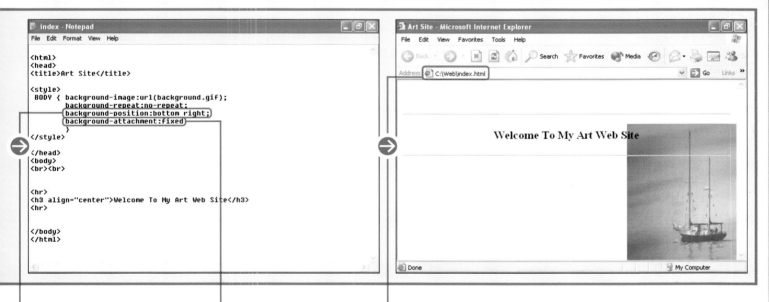

⑥ Type **background-position:?;**, replacing ? with the position of the background image.

⑦ Type **background-attachment:fixed**.

⑧ Save your Web page.

⑨ Type the location of the Web page in your Web browser address bar.

⑩ Press Enter.

○ The background image displays.

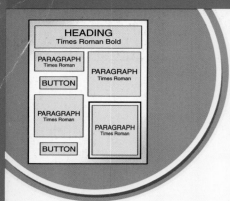

Modify
TEXT APPEARANCE

You can alter the characteristics, and thus the look and layout, of the text that displays on your Web page. You modify how the text appears with the style attribute, which you place in the tag that encloses the text you want to modify.

You align text into a column using the width value to contain the text's width. You use the text-align property in conjunction with the width property to align the text in the column. You can align the text using the values left, right and justify, depending on the type of text alignment you want.

You can easily change any text to upper or lowercase, regardless of the case of the text enclosed by the tag. The text-transform: property with the uppercase or lowercase value changes the case of the text.

Sometimes you need to raise certain items, such as copyright and registered symbols, slightly higher than the preceding text. You vertically align text using the vertical-align: property. A value of super raises the text while a value of sub lowers the text from the original position of the text.

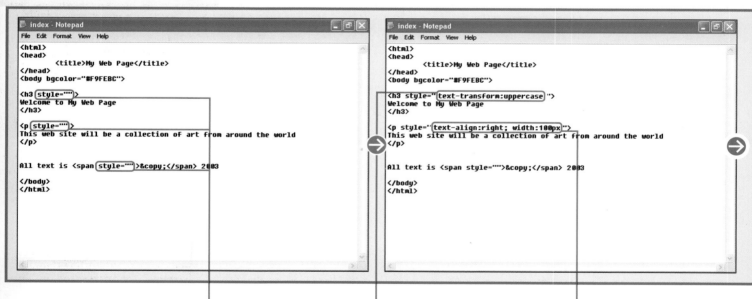

① Open or create a Web page that contains text elements.

② Add the style attribute to the tags that display the text you want to modify.

③ To change the case of the text, type **text-transform:?**, replacing ? with the case of the text.

④ To align text into a column, type **text-align:?; width:#**, replacing ? with the type of alignment and # with the width of the column.

Caution! ☀

Older browsers may not
understand the style information and
the text modification you want to apply. If
a Web browser does not support the style
attribute, then the text displays unformatted.

Apply It! ☀

The vertical-align property has many useful values that
can align text vertically with a line of text

DIFFICULTY LEVEL

Vertical-Align Properties	
Property	*Alignment*
baseline	Bottom of a line
sub	Subscript
super	Superscript
top	The top of the tallest character in the same line
text-top	The top of the tallest character in the selected line
middle	The center of the line
bottom	The bottom of the tallest character in the same line
text-bottom	The bottom of the tallest character in the selected line

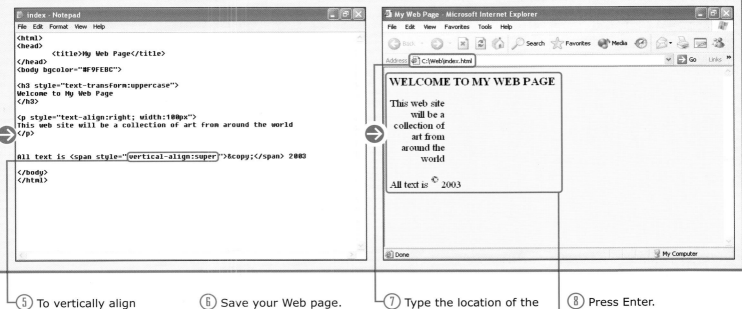

⑤ To vertically align text, type **vertical-align:?**, replacing ? with the type of alignment.

⑥ Save your Web page.

⑦ Type the location of the Web page in your Web browser address bar.

⑧ Press Enter.
○ The modified text displays.

INDEX

Symbols

INDEX

INDEX

INDEX